UNDERSTANDING EAST ASIA'S ECONOMIC "MIRACLES"

Key Issues in Asian Studies, No. 3

AAS Resources for Teaching About Asia

Understanding East Asia's Economic "Miracles"

Zhiqun Zhu

Association for Asian Studies, Inc.
1021 East Huron Street
Ann Arbor, MI 48104 USA
www.asian-studies.org

Published by:
Association for Asian Studies, Inc.
1021 East Huron Street
Ann Arbor, Michigan 48104 USA
www.asian-studies.org

Library of Congress Cataloging-in-Publication Data

Zhu, Zhiqun.
Understanding East Asia's economic miracles / Zhiqun Zhu.
    p. cm. — (Key issues in Asian studies ; no. 3)
Includes bibliographical references.
ISBN 978-0-924304-54-5 (pbk.: alk. paper) 1. East Asia—Economic conditions—Case studies. 2. East Asia—Economic policy—Case studies. I. Title.

HC460.5.Z545 2009
330.95--dc22

2009006197

Front Cover: Lujiazui Financial District with Jinmao Tower, the Oriental Pearl TV Tower and other skyscrapers in Pudong, the Huangpu River, and Puxi, Shanghai, China, August 2008. © Imaginechina.

Back Cover: A Buddhist statue gazing at the cityscape of Seoul, South Korea.

ABOUT THE AUTHOR

ZHIQUN ZHU, PhD, is John D. and Catherine T. MacArthur Chair in East Asian Politics and an associate professor of political science and international relations at Bucknell University in Pennsylvania. His teaching and research interests focus on East Asian and Chinese politics and international political economy. His recent publications include *U.S.–China Relations in the 21st Century: Power Transition and Peace* (London and New York: Routledge, 2006), and *Global Studies: China, 13th edition* (Dubuque, IA: McGraw-Hill, 2009).

To my mother

and

to the memory of my father (1932–2008)

ABOUT "KEY ISSUES IN ASIAN STUDIES"

Key Issues in Asian Studies (*KIAS*) is a series of booklets engaging major cultural and historical themes in the Asian experience. *KIAS* booklets complement the Association for Asian Studies teaching journal, *Education About Asia*, and serve as vital educational materials that are both accessible and affordable for classroom use.

KIAS booklets tackle broad subjects or major events in an introductory but compelling style appropriate for survey courses. Although authors of the series have distinguished themselves as scholars as well as teachers, the prose style employed in *KIAS* booklets is accessible for broad audiences. This series is particularly intended for teachers and undergraduates at two- and four-year colleges as well as advanced high school students and secondary school teachers engaged in teaching Asian studies in a comparative framework.

For further information about *Key Issues in Asian Studies* booklets, *Education About Asia*, or the Association for Asian Studies, please visit www.asian-studies.org.

Prospective authors interested in *Key Issues in Asian Studies* or *Education About Asia* are encouraged to contact:

Lucien Ellington
University of Tennessee at Chattanooga
Tel: (423) 425-2118
Fax (423) 425-5441
E-Mail: Lucien-Ellington@utc.edu
www.asian-studies.org/EAA

Editor's Introduction

Marcus Noland is a Senior Fellow with the Washington-based Peterson Institute for International Economics and is internationally recognized for his work on East Asia. In a Fall 2005 *Education About Asia* interview, Noland perfectly captured the post-war dynamism of the region with the following personal anecdote about his wife:

> *"In 1963, the year of her birth, per capita incomes in my wife's country, Ghana, exceeded those in South Korea. Today South Korean incomes are eight times those in Ghana."*

Since World War II, East Asian countries have been world leaders in economic growth and rising standards of living. In *Understanding East Asia's Economic "Miracles,"* Professor Zhu does a masterful job of lucidly describing the economic rise of the region in accessible, jargon-free prose that is comprehensible to survey-level students as well as to professors and teachers who have little or no background in political economy or economics. Zhu also quite competently introduces non-specialists to some of the controversies surrounding the question of how East Asia has become materially prosperous in recent times. I consider it an honor to have the privilege to have worked with Professor Zhu on this publication.

This booklet would also not have been possible without the helpful comments of Robert Angel, Andrew Oros, and Richard Rice, who served as reviewers of the project in its various stages. Also, I am deeply grateful to the AAS Publications Board (and in particular, Martha Selby) and to AAS Publications Manager, Jonathan Wilson, for their strong support.

Lucien Ellington
Series Editor: Key Issues in Asian Studies

ACKNOWLEDGEMENTS

I am grateful to a number of people who have helped me to make the publication of this booklet possible. First of all, I wish to thank Lucien Ellington, Editor of *Education About Asia* and the "Key Issues in Asian Studies" (KIAS) series, for finding the value in my proposal and for encouraging me to take up the challenge to write the booklet. I am very fortunate to have worked with Lucien and to publish the first booklet in the *KIAS* series under his editorship.

Jonathan Wilson, Publications and Website Manager of the Association for Asian Studies, has overseen the publication of the booklet and has been extremely responsive, meticulous, and efficient. Janet Opdyke, copyeditor for the booklet, carefully read through the manuscript and polished it. Janet's hard work definitely makes the booklet more readable. I also wish to thank the three reviewers for their useful comments and helpful suggestions. All the above individuals have helped to improve the quality of the booklet, but they are not responsible for any mistakes.

As usual, my family has been very patient and supportive during my writing of this booklet. Zhimin, Julia, and Sophia bring me much love and joy every day. I am lucky to have their unconditional support.

Zhiqun Zhu
Lewisburg, Pennsylvania
February 2009

CONTENTS

LIST OF ABBREVIATIONS

APEC	Asia-Pacific Economic Cooperation
CNOOC	China National Offshore Oil Company, Ltd.
DPJ	Democratic Party of Japan
DPP	Democratic Progressive Party
DPRK	Democratic People's Republic of Korea
FDI	foreign direct investment
FILP	Fiscal Investment and Loan Plan
GATT	General Agreement on Tariffs and Trade
GDP	gross domestic product
GNP	gross national product
IMD	International Institute for Management Development
IMF	International Monetary Fund
IPO	initial public offering
IT	information technology
JCRR	Joint Commission on Rural Reconstruction
KMT	Kuomintang
LCD	liquid crystal display
LDP	Liberal Democratic Party
MCI	Ministry of Commerce and Industry
METI	Ministry of Economy, Trade, and Industry
MITI	Ministry of International Trade and Industry
MM	Ministry of Munitions
MOF	Ministry of Finance
NIE	newly industrializing economy
OECD	Organization for Economic Cooperation and Development
PPP	purchasing power parity
PRC	People's Republic of China
ROC	Republic of China
ROK	Republic of Korea
SCAP	Supreme Commander of the Allied Powers

SEZ	special economic zone
SOE	state-owned enterprise
TRA	Taiwan Relations Act
UNCTAD	United Nations Conference on Trade and Development
UNESCO	United Nations Educational, Scientific, and Cultural Organization
UNIKOTECH	Unification of Korean Technologies
WHO	World Health Organization
WTO	World Trade Organization

MODERN EAST ASIAN
HISTORY TIMELINE

1839–42	Opium War
1853–54	Commodore Matthew Perry visits Japan
1868	Meiji Restoration begins in Japan
1894–95	First Sino-Japanese War
1895	Japan defeats Qing dynasty China and colonizes Taiwan
1904–05	Russo-Japanese War
1910	Japan colonizes the Korean Peninsula, Korea's Choson dynasty ends
1911	Republic of China is established
1931	Japan creates the puppet state of Manchukuo in Manchuria
1937	Japan invades China and captures the capital city of Nanjing
1945	Japan surrenders at the end of World War II
	Chinese Civil War resumes
1947	Japan ratifies a new constitution and adopts land reform
1948	Republic of Korea (ROK) and the Democratic People's Republic of Korea (DPRK) are established
1949	People's Republic of China (PRC) is established
	Ministry of International Trade and Industry (MITI) is formed in Japan
	Land reform begins in Taiwan
1950–53	Korean War
1955	Japan's Liberal Democratic Party (LDP) is formed
1958–61	"Great Leap Forward" in China
1964	Tokyo Summer Olympics
1966–76	"Cultural Revolution" in China
1971	PRC enters the United Nations, replacing Taiwan
1972	United States returns Okinawa to Japan
	President Richard Nixon visits China
1978	Deng Xiaoping's reform and opening-up policies are implemented
1979	Four Special Economic Zones (SEZ) are established in Southern China
	PRC and the U.S. establish diplomatic relations

1980	Kwangju uprising in South Korea
1987	Martial law is lifted in Taiwan
1988	Seoul Summer Olympics
1989	Tiananmen Square demonstrations
	Asia-Pacific Economic Cooperation (APEC) is founded
1990s	Famines in North Korea
1991	Japanese economic "bubble" bursts, initiating the "lost decade"
1996	South Korea is admitted to the Organization for Economic Cooperation and Development (OECD)
1997	Asian financial crisis
	Hong Kong is returned to China
2000	Kuomintang loses power to the Democratic Progressive Party (DPP) in Taiwan
	First Inter-Korean Summit between South Korean President Kim Dae-jung and North Korean leader Kim Jong-il
2001	China enters the World Trade Organization (WTO)
	Ministry of Economy, Trade, and Industry (METI) replaces MITI
2003	Six-Party Talks over North Korea's nuclear program are launched in Beijing
2004	Protection of private property is written into the Chinese Constitution
2005	Agricultural taxes—which have existed for two-thousand years—are abolished in China
2007	The PRC Property Law goes into effect
	The Liberal Democratic Party (LDP) loses majority in upper house of the Japanese Diet
2007–08	South Koreans protest U.S.-ROK free trade agreement and U.S. beef imports
2008	Beijing Summer Olympics
	Global financial crisis
	The Chinese mainland and Taiwan start direct air and sea transport and postal services—the first time since the two sides split after the civil war in 1949
	Former ROC President Chen Shui-bian is arrested and indicted for forgery, money-laundering, and the misuse of public funds
2009	China announces its plan to provide universal health care by 2011

1

INTRODUCTION

Since the end of World War II no region in the world has been so dynamic as East Asia, where one nation after another has created remarkable economic "miracles." First Japan rose from the devastation of the Pacific War like a phoenix coming back to life and quickly became the second-largest economy in the world, next only to the United States. Then the Republic of Korea (South Korea, ROK) and Taiwan, both former colonies of Japan, experienced economic takeoffs under authoritarian regimes before moving toward full democracy, achieving both economic and political marvels in a relatively short period of time. Finally, in the late 1970s Deng Xiaoping, realizing that China was falling far behind many of its neighbors in living standards, decided to initiate market reforms in the countryside and gradually opened China's door to Western investment and technology, policies that pushed China onto a fast development track and helped turn it into an economic powerhouse at the beginning of the twenty-first century. Collectively, East Asia's impressive economic growth and the social progress achieved in the six decades after World War II are unparalleled in human history.

The word "miracle" suggests some sort of divine intervention. In East Asia, there has been no such divine power. East Asia's economic "miracles" have come from decades of hard work by the people of East Asia. These achievements have also been helped by favorable international and domestic conditions, sound government policies, and far-sighted individual leaders.

The so-called "flying geese pattern" vividly describes the post–World War II economic development of East Asia, with Japan as the leading goose followed by the four "little dragons" or "little tigers" (South Korea, Taiwan, Singapore, and Hong Kong) and other economies. In 1960, Japan and the rest of Asia accounted for only 5 percent of the world's gross national product (GNP) compared to 37 percent for North America. By the early twenty-first century, they accounted for roughly 30 percent of world GNP, about the same share as those held by North America and Europe.

China's profound economic and social transformations since the late 1970s, especially its spectacular surge in the first decade of the twenty-first century, have reignited scholarly and policy interest in East Asia's development models. Has China followed the same development trajectory as other East Asian economies? Is the People's Republic of China (PRC) replaying the East Asian "miracles" performed earlier by Japan, South Korea, Taiwan, and others?

Despite the extraordinary economic growth of post–World War II East Asia, what happened in the 1990s cast considerable doubt on the vitality of the often touted "East Asian model." Japan's decade-long economic stagnation that began in the early 1990s and the 1997–98 financial crisis in some of the East Asian and Southeast Asian economies led many people to ask what was wrong with the highly regarded development miracle in East Asia. Is such development sustainable? What is the current status of these economies? Are global resources sufficient to sustain further growth in East Asia and elsewhere?

This booklet, through an historical and comparative study of the economic performances of Japan, South Korea, and China (including both mainland China and Taiwan), examines all the major explanations and analyses in accounting for East Asia's economic "miracles." It also discusses the implications for other developing economies as they emulate East Asia's success story. It is intended to help readers better understand the East Asian development experience, including both its strengths and its weaknesses.

What powerful forces have fueled East Asia's rapid growth since World War II? Is there a singular East Asian model of economic development? What are the differences and similarities in the development paths of Japan, South Korea, Taiwan, and the PRC? What is the relationship between economic growth and type of political regime? Can East Asia's high-performing development strategies be copied by other developing regions? This booklet provides a comprehensive survey of East Asian nations' post-World War II development from historical, cultural, institutional, political, economic, and international perspectives. It will be helpful for understanding these successful economies and the driving forces behind them. It will also be significant for other developing nations as they attempt to mimic East Asia's growth trajectory.

This booklet can be used at a variety of lower-level undergraduate classes in political science, government, economics, history, and Asian studies. It will be especially germane to introductory or survey courses such as East Asian Political Economy, Comparative Politics of East Asia, and Modern East Asian

History. Since it has been written as an introductory reading on the topic, it should also be appropriate for advanced high school classes such as advanced placement courses in world history, world politics, and economics.

Diversity and vitality are two distinctive features of East Asian nations. To understand these economies, it is important first of all to recognize that, although they enjoy some similarities in economic strategies, they differ greatly in their economic histories, political systems, political cultures, and foreign relations. An analysis of both internal and external factors is needed to explain East Asia's economic "miracles" after World War II. Chapters 2 through 4 examine post–World War II development in Japan, South Korea, and China (both the PRC and Taiwan). Chapter 5 systematically compares and contrasts these cases. Chapter 6 summarizes the discussion and develops a comprehensive framework for better understanding the economic "miracles" of East Asia.

2

JAPAN AND THE "DEVELOPMENTAL STATE" MODEL

J apan was a relatively closed society in the first half of the nineteenth century. American Commodore Matthew C. Perry's July 1853 and February 1854 visits to Japan marked the official, albeit forced, opening of Japan to American and Western trade and influence. Through the Convention of Kanagawa and the subsequent United States–Japan Treaty of Amity and Commerce, America's gunboat diplomacy helped integrate Japan into the Western world and create a future economic giant in the East.

In an effort to avoid the fate of colonization or exploitation that China was suffering, Japan launched an ambitious drive to industrialize and modernize. The Meiji Restoration, which began in 1868, was in effect Japan's modernization and industrialization movement. Under the slogan "Enrich the country, strengthen the military" (fukoku kyōhei, 富国強兵), Japan mobilized all its resources and quickly rose to become a military power by the end of the nineteenth century. The Japanese economy was no longer predominantly agricultural, and Japan easily defeated an enfeebled and declining Qing dynasty China in the first Sino-Japanese War (1894–95), which permanently changed the power structure in East Asia and accelerated the fall of the last dynasty in China. Meiji leaders' aim to turn the country into a power equal to the West had become a reality by the early twentieth century with the end of the unequal treaties that had been imposed on Japan.

Japan was essentially given a free hand to grow and expand as the European powers were busy competing with one another while the United States stood on the sidelines of great power politics at the end of the nineteenth century and the beginning of the twentieth. Japan's ambitions in Manchuria and Korea collided with those of Russia, a great European power. Japan's fledgling navy surprisingly defeated Russia in the Russo-Japanese War (1904–05). In the Treaty of Portsmouth, signed on September 5, 1905, Russia recognized the Korean Peninsula as part of the Japanese sphere of influence and agreed to

Shinto Shrine in Atomic Ruins, Nagasaki, Japan, October 1945. Photo courtesy U.S. Marine Corps.

evacuate Manchuria. Japan annexed Korea in 1910 with scant protest from other powers. In World War I, Japan seized German possessions in Asia, including the Shandong Peninsula in China. In 1931, Japan invaded Manchuria and established the puppet government of Manchukuo (Manzhouguo). By 1937, Japan had occupied many other parts of China, including the capital city of Nanjing (Nanking). It also invaded much of Southeast Asia in an attempt to create a "Greater East Asia Co-prosperity Sphere."

The Pacific War, with the participation of the United States, ended Japan's militarism, which had brought disaster to much of Asia, including Japan itself. The United States dropped atomic bombs on Hiroshima and Nagasaki on August 6 and August 9, 1945, respectively, leading to Japan's official surrender to the Allied Powers on August 15, 1945.

Japan's economic reconstruction began shortly after the war. However, to label the country's high growth rate following World War II a "miracle" underrates the transformation of Japan's economy which began in the nineteenth century and the expansion of heavy industry during the 1930s. Japan already had a highly developed military and industry before World War

II, which distinguished it from other East Asian countries. It is not surprising that Japan created the first economic "miracle" in East Asia from the ashes of the war. From the early 1950s until the beginning of the 1990s, Japan's GNP grew at rates double those of most other members of the Organization for Economic Cooperation and Development (OECD), its share of world exports quadrupled, and its economy leapfrogged from twentieth in the world to second. Amazed by its rapid growth, America's renowned scholar Ezra Vogel called Japan the "number one" country in the world at the end of the 1970s.[1] Yet the Japanese economy experienced stagnation during the so-called lost decade of the 1990s before it was able to slowly recover. What explains Japan's impressive postwar economic growth, its setbacks, and its resurgence? Does the country's economic performance during the 1990s, including the years following the 1997 Asian financial crisis, spell the end of the Japanese "miracle"? Factors in Japan's economic development—including effective national policies such as the *Yoshida Doctrine* and the 1947 land reform, U.S. economic aid and military support, the Korean War, and the country's postwar cohesion, culture, and relationships with the international community—must all be addressed if we are to understand Japan's postwar development path.

THE YOSHIDA DOCTRINE AND THE 1955 SYSTEM

The *Yoshida Doctrine* refers to the reconstruction policy devised by Japan's first postwar Prime Minister, Yoshida Shigeru (1878–1967). Yoshida served as Prime Minister from 1946 to 1947 and again from 1948 to 1954. The *Yoshida Doctrine* advocated adopting the U.S. stance on security and international relations issues and relying on U.S. military protection in order to allow Japan to focus its resources on economic production and the creation of a skilled labor force. Yoshida's aim was to focus all available resources on Japan's economic recovery while leaving its military defense to the United States. Japan would not spend more than 1 percent of its gross domestic product (GDP) on the military. In fact, attempts by the United States to persuade Japan to increase its military expenditures were rejected by Yoshida on the basis of the country's pacifist postwar constitution, in particular Article 9, under which Japan "renounces war as

Japan's first postwar Prime Minister, Yoshida Shigeru.

a sovereign right of the nation and the threat or use of force as means of settling international disputes. " Yoshida's policies were greatly elaborated by his successors over the next several decades into a full-blown national strategy, and the *Yoshida Doctrine* served as the basic tenet of Japanese foreign policy in the postwar years and during the Cold War.

While the *Yoshida Doctrine* set the tone for Japan's postwar reconstruction, the Korean War (1950–53) boom proved to be an unexpected shot in the arm and made it possible for Japan to make a fast economic recovery almost at a single stroke. The economic boom resulting from the Korean War was triggered by the special procurements earnings from U.S. military expenditures and by the sudden rise in exports that accompanied the expansion of world trade after June 1950.

The term *1955 system* refers to the continuous dominance of the Liberal Democratic Party (LDP) over the Japanese political economy since 1955. The LDP was founded by different conservative political forces in 1955 and oversaw Japan's economic development after it regained its sovereignty from the Allied (principally American) Forces in 1952. Whereas the LDP shared the neomercantilist view that Japan should become a competitive economic power, the party had to manage at least two different conflicts. On the one hand, big businesses, elite bureaucrats, and politicians wanted to create large, internationally competitive firms through favorable industrial policies and fiscal responsibility. On the other hand, the small businessmen and farmers who were key party constituents preferred local protection and subsidies. The LDP managed to reconcile these two competing interest groups by adopting an industrial policy of upgrading technologies and penetrating foreign markets while protecting the home turf from foreign competition.[2] With a secure domestic base, Japanese firms enjoyed a comparative advantage over foreign competitors.

The LDP's strength was based on an enduring coalition of business, agriculture, professional groups, and other interests. Elite bureaucrats collaborated closely with the party and interest groups in drafting and implementing economic policies. The system functioned efficiently as a locus for matching interest group money and votes with bureaucratic power and expertise. This arrangement resulted in problems such as corruption, but the party could claim credit for helping to create economic growth and a stable, middle-class Japan.

The *1955 system* ensured the continuity of Japanese economic and foreign policies from the 1950s until the early 1990s. In the August 1993 election of the Diet, the Japanese parliament, the LDP lost as a result of Japan's economic

8

decline, scandals associated with party leaders, the lack of long-awaited reform programs, and factional rivalries within the party. The downfall of the LDP after thirty-eight years of rule is referred to as the "collapse of the *1955 system* or 1955 setup" in Japanese political history.

In 1994, the Japan Socialist Party and New Party Sakigake left the ruling coalition and joined the LDP in the opposition. With the help of the Socialist Party and New Party, the LDP was returned to power, although it allowed a Socialist to occupy the Prime Minister's chair. By 1996, the LDP was able to return to power as a majority party. It was practically unopposed until 1998, when the opposition Democratic Party of Japan (DPJ) was formed. Since then, the opposition has gained momentum, especially in the 2003 and 2004 parliamentary elections.

In the July 2007 House of Councilors (the upper house of the Diet) elections, the LDP suffered a huge defeat and lost its majority for the first time in history while the DPJ managed to gain the largest margin in the upper house since its formation in 1998. The LDP was able to hold the majority in the House of Representatives (the lower house of the Diet) but had to share a coalition government with the conservative Buddhist New Komeito.

ZAIBATSU AND KEIRETSU

Zaibatsu and *keiretsu* played crucial roles in Japan's economic development and postwar reconstruction. *Zaibatsu* (財閥) refers to industrial and financial business conglomerates in the empire of Japan, whose influence and size allowed them to control significant parts of the Japanese economy from the Meiji period until the end of World War II. Very large *zaibatsu* such as the "Big Four" (Mitsubishi, Mitsui, Sumitomo, and Yasuda) were the most significant groups historically, having roots that stemmed from the Edo period (also known as the Tokugawa period, 1603–1868).

After the Russo-Japanese War, a number of so-called second-tier *zaibatsu* emerged, mostly as the result of conglomeration and/or the winning of lucrative military contracts. Some of the more famous second-tier *zaibatsu* were the Okura, Furukawa, and Nakajima groups. All prospered in the boom years of World War II.

The American occupation dismantled the largest *zaibatsu* in the late 1940s, but the companies formed from the dismantling were soon reintegrated. The new corporations were linked through share purchases to form horizontally-integrated alliances across many industries. A *keiretsu* (系列, *system* or *series*) is a set of companies with interlocking business relationships and shareholdings.

9

The prototypical *keiretsu* appeared in Japan following World War II. When possible, *keiretsu* companies would supply one another, making the alliances vertically integrated as well, assisted by a major bank in the group.

In addition to *keiretsu*, the Japanese economy during the postwar years was characterized by cooperation among manufacturers, suppliers, distributors, and banks; powerful enterprise unions; cozy relationships between businesses and government bureaucrats; and the guarantee of lifetime employment (*shushin koyo* 终身雇用) in big corporations and highly unionized blue-collar factories.

There are two types of *keiretsu*: vertical and horizontal. Vertical *keiretsu* illustrate the organization and relationships within a company (e.g., all factors in the production of a certain product are connected), while horizontal *keiretsu* illustrate relationships between member firms and industries, normally centered around a bank and trading company. Both are complexly woven together and help sustain each other.

A *keiretsu*'s bank lent money to the member companies and held equity positions in them. Each central bank had great control over the companies in the *keiretsu*, overseeing their activities and bailing them out if necessary. One effect of this was to minimize hostile takeovers in Japan because no single entity could challenge the power of the banks.

The close relationship between *zaibatsu/keiretsu* and the bureaucracy is another feature of Japan's economic policy, the so-called "developmental state" model. A recognized weakness of the closely knit relationship is its vulnerability to corruption and other economic scandals. Economic dominance and conservative research and development policies made it difficult for startups and new industries to emerge in the 1990s. Japan has a weak initial public offering (IPO) structure that considerably inhibits its growth potential. The IPO is the process of taking a privately owned company public by listing its shares on a stock exchange. A weak IPO process makes it difficult for companies to aggressively compete in cutting-edge technology markets. Another weakness of this model is the fact that government bureaucrats often have a difficult time predicting the future.

Private sector entrepreneurs and corporate leaders helped enhance Japan's postwar economic growth and global competitiveness. For example, Honda Sōichirō (本田宗一郎), founder of the Honda Motor Company, Ltd., started his auto repair business in 1928 at the age of twenty-two. In 1948, he began producing motorcycles as president of the Honda Motor Company and turned the company into a billion-dollar multinational that produced the best-selling motorcycles in the world. In 1959, Honda went global and opened its first dealership in the United States. Toyoda Kiichiro (豊田喜一郎), founder of the Toyota Motor Corporation, made a strategic decision in 1937 to transform the Toyoda Loom Works, which he inherited from his father, into an automobile manufacturing facility, which was considered a risky business at the time. A few years after he died in 1952, his cousin, Toyoda Eiji, became head of the Toyota Motor Corporation, successfully expanded its business worldwide, and launched Japan's most prominent luxury vehicle brand, Lexus.

THE JAPANESE "MIRACLE"

Postwar inflation, unemployment, and shortages in all areas seemed overwhelming at first. Yet Japan experienced a phenomenal period of economic growth spurred partly by U.S. investment during the Korean War (1950–53) but mainly by the Japanese government's economic interventionism. Many people give full credit to Japan's Ministry of International Trade and Industry (MITI) for its role in the Japanese "miracle," although this claim remains controversial.

The "miracle" continued to unfold during the "Golden Sixties." In 1965, Japan's nominal GNP was estimated at just over $91 billion. Fifteen years later it had soared to a record $1.065 trillion.

While the *Yoshida Doctrine* guided Japan's postwar economic and security policies, Prime Minister Ikeda Hayato (1960–64) has been described by some as the single most important figure in Japan's rapid growth during the 1960s. Under the leadership of Ikeda, a former minister of MITI, the Japanese government undertook an ambitious "income-doubling plan." Ikeda's plan predicted a 7.2 percent growth rate that would double the GNP over ten years, but by the second half of the 1960s average growth had climbed to an astounding 11.6 percent. Ikeda also actively promoted Japan's exports. In 1960, French president Charles De Gaulle famously referred to him as "that transistor salesman."[3] Ikeda furthered Japan's global economic integration by joining the General Agreement on Tariffs and Trade (GATT, the predecessor of the World Trade Organization [WTO]) in 1963 and the International Monetary Fund (IMF) and OECD in 1964.

Prime Minister Ikeda Hayato was credited with Japan's rapid growth in the 1960s.

11

Hosting the 1964 Summer Olympic Games reflected Japan's commitment to doubling GNP, as well as symbolizing its full reentry into the international community as a peaceful and fair player. By the time Ikeda left office, Japan's GNP was growing at a phenomenal rate of 13.9 percent annually.

Japan has few natural resources, and trade helps it earn the foreign exchange needed to purchase raw materials for its economy. Manufacturing, construction, distribution, real estate, services, and communications are Japan's major industries. Today agriculture makes up only about 2 percent of the GNP. The most important agricultural product is rice. Japan's main export goods are cars, electronic devices, and computers. Its most important trading partner has traditionally been the United States, which still imports about one-fifth of all Japanese exports. However, since the mid-2000s China has been Japan's largest trading partner. Japan has a large surplus in its export-import balance. The most important import goods are raw materials such as oil, foodstuffs, and wood.

The government played an effective leadership role in Japan's economic recovery. The Japanese "miracle" was achieved as a result of "guided capitalism" in which the state was heavily involved in economic activities and indeed provided official guidance in economic decision making to businesses.

WHAT IS THE "DEVELOPMENTAL STATE" MODEL?

Since all states intervene in their economies, the question to pose is how and to what extent does each government excercise its influence. *Developmental state* is a term used by international political economy scholars to refer to state-led macroeconomic planning in post-World War II East Asia. A developmental state intervenes directly in the economy through a variety of means to promote the growth of new industries and to reduce the dislocations caused by shifts in investment and profits from old to new industries. The developmental state model emphasizes the critical role of the state or government in promoting economic growth. Japan is considered the best example of such a state-guided economic system.

The concept of the developmental state was first articulated in Chalmers Johnson's 1982 book *MITI and the Japanese Miracle*, in which he recounted how MITI, the Ministry of International Trade and Industry, worked consistently and diligently to promote economic growth.[4] This strong-state model of capitalism is vastly different from the liberal market system represented by the United States and Great Britain, where the state is supposed to stay away from market operations (laissez-faire) except in a regulatory capacity; it is also different from the purely state-dominated command economies of the former communist states. Johnson does not completely reject alternative explanations for the Japanese "miracle," but he decidedly gives the most weight to the role of the state and its industrial policies, declaring, "The significant difference is that in Japan the state's role in the economy is shared with the private sector, and both the public and private sectors have perfected means to make the market work for developmental goals" (viii). In the West, France has pursued a similar policy.

From its beginnings as the Ministry of Commerce and Industry (MCI) in 1925 to its transformation as the Ministry of Munitions (MM) in 1943, its reemergence as the MCI in 1945, and its reorganization as MITI in 1949, Japan's key economic bureaucracy has played a leading role in the nation's growth. In 2001, MITI's role was taken over by the newly created Ministry of Economy, Trade, and Industry (METI).

Established in 1949, MITI formalized cooperation between the Japanese government and private industry. It coordinated various industries, including the emerging *keiretsu*, toward the intersection of national production goals and private economic interests. It also boosted the industrial sector by untying the importation of technology from the importation of other goods. Realizing the importance of technology in development, MITI's Foreign Capital Law, passed in 1950, granted the power to negotiate the prices and conditions of technology importation. This allowed it to promote industries it deemed promising. Productivity was greatly improved through new equipment, management, and standardization.

With the abolition of the Economic Stabilization Board and the Foreign Exchange Control Board in August 1952, MITI gained the ability to regulate imports. Its establishment of the Japan Development Bank in 1951 also provided the private sector with low-cost capital for long-term growth. The bank provided access to the Fiscal Investment and Loan Plan (FILP), a massive pooling of individual postal and national savings accounts. At the time, FILP controlled four times the savings of the world's largest commercial bank.

Market forces alone could not produce the levels of growth Japanese leaders desired. While MITI may be an economic bureaucracy, it is not a bureaucracy of economists. In fact, many of its officials hold law or public administration degrees from Japan's top universities. The Japanese perfected the government-business relationship and employed it in more sectors than other capitalist nations. Japan's postwar political system has often been characterized as an "iron triangle" of conservative LDP politicians, big businesses, and elite bureaucrats.

Japan's developmental state model has utilized elements from both the market and command economies to its advantage. Its state-guided economy demonstrates that a national government can use broad policy control over the economy to offset the disadvantage of late industrialization without the loss of private initiatives and incentives. An aggressive policy of government control over resource allocations for sectors such as agriculture and energy can accomplish a great deal in the early stages of economic development.

Johnson may have exaggerated the role of MITI while ignoring those of other ministries, especially the Ministry of Finance (MOF). In addition, the Japanese government is more democratic than Johnson describes. Like other ministries, MITI is not dictatorial but responds to public demand. The important role of the state in Japan's postwar economic development was also studied by other scholars, including T. J. Pempel, Richard Katz, and Meredith Woo-Cumings.[5]

After the 1997 Asian financial crisis, the strong state model became associated with crony capitalism in many people's minds. *Crony capitalism* is a pejorative term for an allegedly capitalist economy in which success in business depends on close relationships between businessmen and government officials. It is typified by favoritism in the distribution of legal contracts, government grants, special tax breaks, and so forth. However, some scholars think that Japan's development in the 1990s was actually a departure from the original "developmental state" model.

THE INTERNATIONAL ENVIRONMENT AND U.S. AID

Any explanation of postwar Japan's economic development would be incomplete without a mention of the role of the United States. The post–World War II world was immediately plunged into the Cold War between capitalist and communist governments. During the occupation, the United States successfully demilitarized and democratized Japan, turning it into a key ally in Asia. The American government, under the auspices of General Douglas MacArthur, Supreme Commander of the Allied Powers (SCAP), played a crucial role in Japan's initial economic recovery.

The 1950s stands out as a distinctive era in U.S.-Japan relations. In 1950, the two countries began negotiations to end the state of war between them. In these negotiations, the U.S. government also desired a Japanese commitment to the American side in the Cold War while the Japanese government sought an American guarantee of Japan's external defense. The result was the conclusion of two treaties in 1951 (which entered into force the following year): the

General Douglas MacArthur and Emperor Hirohito, at their first meeting, at the U.S. Embassy, Tokyo, September 27, 1945. The American government, under the auspices of General MacArthur, Supreme Commander of the Allied Powers (SCAP), played a crucial role in Japan's initial economic recovery. Photo by U.S. Army photographer Lt. Gaetano Faillace.

multilateral San Francisco Peace Treaty, which brought the occupation to a close; and the bilateral U.S.-Japan Security Treaty, in which the United States pledged to maintain its military forces in and around Japan.

Following World War II, the United States provided reconstruction assistance to Japan. According to a study by the Congressional Research Service, total U.S. assistance to Japan in 1946–52 was roughly $15.2 billion in constant 2005 dollars, of which 77 percent was in the form of grants and 23 percent in loans. However, American aid to Japan was about half of what it provided for Germany, which totaled $29.3 billion in constant 2005 dollars from 1946 to 1952.[6]

Almost a third of U.S. assistance went to categories that would contribute directly to Japan's economic recovery (industrial materials, including machinery and raw goods; petroleum and petroleum products; and transportation, vehicles, and equipment). Most of the rest went for agricultural equipment, foodstuffs, and food supplies with smaller amounts spent on medical and sanitary supplies, education, and clothing. The United States had tense relations with both the Soviet Union and the People's Republic of China for most of the Cold War, which made Japan strategically very important to the United States. A secure international environment protected by the United States and generous economic assistance helped facilitate Japan's economic takeoff in the postwar years.

Hostilities on the Korean Peninsula further boosted Japan's economy in 1950 because the United States paid the Japanese government large sums for special military procurements. These payments amounted to 27 percent of Japan's total export trade that year. The Korean War brought a flood of American war orders, which temporarily alleviated Japan's chronic foreign trade imbalance. During the Korean War, SCAP departed and full sovereignty was returned to the government of Japan, except for Okinawa, which was returned to Japanese control in 1972. The United States also insisted, over British opposition, that Japan be admitted to the GATT as a "temporary member." American sponsorship of Japan's admission to important international economic organizations, the United States' decision to allow Japan access to its market without demanding commensurate access to Japan's market for U.S. goods, and Japan's easy access to U.S. technology were all helpful during reconstruction.

THE JAPANESE BUBBLE AND THE FINANCIAL CRISIS

The state-guided, export-led strategy, despite some setbacks, worked well for Japan until the mid-1980s when the yen began to appreciate sharply after the 1985 Plaza Accord.[7] Between 1986 and 1990, Japan experienced one of the greatest bubble economies in history. It began after the Japanese agreed to demands by other major industrialized nations that they substantially increase the value of the yen in 1985 (it doubled by 1988). When the Ministry of Finance lowered the prime interest rate from 5 percent to a postwar low of 2.5 percent, asset markets predictably skyrocketed. The value of commercially zoned property in central Tokyo, already the most expensive real estate in the world, jumped tenfold by 1989.

The Plaza Accord was meant to reduce Japan's mounting trade surpluses with the United States and other major economies, but it led to a huge bubble in real estate and stock values due to limited investment opportunities. When the bubble burst in 1991, it ushered in a "lost decade" of economic stagnation during which Japan also suffered from the Asian financial crisis in 1997.

The financial crisis gripped much of Asia beginning in the summer of 1997. It started in Thailand where the government decided to float the baht, the Thai currency, and cut its peg to the U.S. dollar after exhaustive efforts to support it in the face of a severe financial overextension partly caused by a real estate bubble. As the crisis spread, most of Southeast Asia and Japan saw slumping currencies, devalued stock and other asset prices, and a precipitous rise in private debt. The Japanese market did not collapse, but it was severely hit. Japan's GNP real growth rate slowed dramatically in 1997, from 5 to 1.6 percent, and sank to recession levels in 1998 due to intense competition from rivals. The unemployment rate reached a record 3.9 percent during the crisis.

The Asian financial crisis also led to more bankruptcies in Japan. In November 1997, Sanyo Securities and Yamaichi Securities (two of Japan's largest brokerages) and Hokkaido Takushoku (its tenth-largest bank) collapsed; shortly afterward Tokyo City Bank, a large regional bank, closed. The U.S. treasury secretary, Robert Rubin, urged Japan to shore up its banking system. In December 1997, Japan announced a series of reflationary measures, including a cut in the income tax. In January 1998, the Diet approved a $228 billion financial stabilization plan. In June 1998, the yen fell to an eight-year low against the U.S. dollar, driving down prices of stocks and currencies around the world. In September 1998, Japan Leasing Corp., a major leasing company, filed for bankruptcy protection. With a debt totaling $16 billion, it was then the largest bankruptcy filing since World War II.

THE JAPANESE ECONOMY AT THE BEGINNING OF THE TWENTY-FIRST CENTURY

In the 1970s and 1980s, Japan was the "next big thing." With a huge foreign exchange reserve, it adopted an investment-led strategy and began to purchase overseas, including capturing such iconic properties as the Rockefeller Center in New York. The United States was weakening in the wake of "the Rising Sun." Ezra Vogel in his 1979 book, *Japan as Number One* analyzed traits that he thought contributed to the Japanese "miracle" such as basic education, low crime rates, a powerful but efficient bureaucracy, and a functioning democracy. Vogel was drawing lessons for America, hoping that it could do better and could respond constructively to the challenges from Japan. By the time his long-awaited 2001 sequel *Is Japan Still Number One?* was published, Japan had fallen to number twenty-one in the global growth competitiveness index ranking, according to the *World Competitiveness Yearbook* published by the Swiss International Institute for Management Development (IMD).[8] Vogel takes up the issue of Japan's lost decade of the 1990s by attributing it to the very system he once praised. Now he provides lessons for Japan and suggests that it "needs a third wave of reforms as forward-thinking and as comprehensive as the reforms instituted in the Meiji era and during the early postwar era" (86). What exactly happened to Japan's development model? What is the current status of the Japanese economy?

Close government-industry cooperation, a strong work ethic, and mastery of high technology continue to help Japan advance with extraordinary speed and maintain one of the largest economies in the world. Its reservoir of industrial leadership and technicians; a well-educated and industrious workforce; relatively high, albeit declining, savings and investment rates; and intensive promotion of industrial development and foreign trade have produced a mature industrial economy.

Japan's overall real economic growth from the 1960s to the 1980s has been called a "miracle": a 10 per cent average in the 1960s, a 5 percent average in the 1970s, and a 4 percent average in the 1980s. Growth slowed markedly in the 1990s with an average growth rate of only 1 percent, largely due to the Bank of Japan's failure to cut interest rates quickly enough to counter the aftereffects of overinvestment during the late 1980s. By late 2005, the economy finally had begun what seems to be a sustained recovery. Growth in GNP that year was 2.8 percent, surpassing the growth rates of the United States and European Union during the same period.

In early 2008, Ota Hiroko, the minister of state for economic and fiscal policy, declared that Japan's economy could no longer be considered first class.[9] Indeed, Japan is facing many challenges in the twenty-first century. The population is aging fast, many companies are losing ground to aggressive Asian rivals, and the desperately needed financial reforms have not been forthcoming.

Japan provides the first example of an economy facing the challenge of producing growth in a society with a decreasing and aging population. The Japanese population peaked in 2005 and has been declining ever since. Studies suggest that the percentage of Japanese age sixty-five and over, which was 19.9 percent of the total population, will rise to 27.8 per cent by 2020 and 29.6 per cent by 2030. Meanwhile, in 2005, the age cohort zero to four years old (which will be the twenty- to twenty-four-year-old group in 2025) was 25 percent smaller than the current cohort of the same age.[10]

Exports have been a key driver of Japan's economic recovery since the late 1990s, but in 2008 they fell for the first time in five years as a result of declining consumer demand in the United States and other countries as

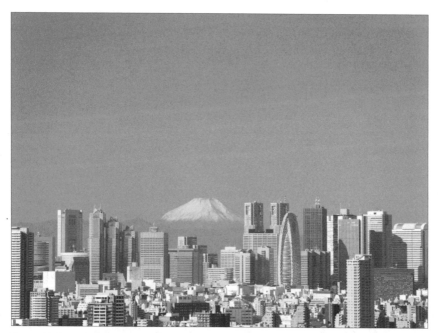

Japan Today—Tokyo with Mount Fuji in the background.

well as strong competition from developing economies, especially China and India. Meanwhile, due to rising oil prices, Japan's imports grew faster than exports and the trade surplus experienced its largest decline since 2001.

However, Japan has remained the second-largest economy in the world (the fourth largest adjusted for purchasing power parity [PPP]) in the first decade of the twenty-first century. The Japanese economy is dynamic and high-tech based. Japan's foreign currency reserve is the second largest in the world after China, and Japan is the second largest foreign holder of U.S. Treasuries after China. The Japanese economy is moving in the direction of greater reliance on market forces and less on government guidance. The Japanese society is beginning to grapple with the implications of its political, economic, and demographic challenges. Issues such as whether more foreign workers should be allowed in and how the role of women in the labor force can be enhanced to increase productivity in a traditionally male-dominated society are seriously debated.

3

SOUTH KOREA: FROM A COLONY TO AN ECONOMIC POWER

The Korean Peninsula was traditional, feudal, agrarian, and isolated from the West until the late nineteenth century. Nicknamed "a shrimp among whales," Korea had always lived in the shadow of great powers. For much of its history, it was essentially a tributary state of imperial China.

The peninsula was a Japanese colony between 1910 and 1945, which brought both exploitation and modernization. Shortly after Japan surrendered, ending the Pacific War, on August 15, 1945, the peninsula was divided into North and South Korea. The United States took control south of the 38th Parallel while the Soviet Union took control of the north. The United Nations called for general elections on the peninsula in 1947, but the North Koreans refused. The Republic of Korea (ROK) was established in the south, and a communist form of government was adopted in the north (officially the Democratic People's Republic of Korea [DPRK]) in 1948. During the 1950–53 Korean War, the two Koreas, each supported by its great power allies, fought a bloody war. An armistice, but not a peace treaty, was signed in 1953—so technically the two Koreas are still at war.

South Korea began with an autocratic government, experimented with limited democracy in 1960–61, took an authoritarian turn in the 1960s, saw increased repression in the 1970s, and began genuine democratization in the late 1980s. With astonishing economic development from the 1960s to the 1980s, South Korea became one of the "Asian tigers." Since the late 1980s, it has also been one of the most vibrant democracies in the world.

THE KOREAN "MIRACLE"

A brief comparison between the two Koreas is contextually useful. The Republic of Korea (South Korea) was established on August 15, 1948, headed by Syngman Rhee, a Princeton-educated, pro-West, nationalist leader. The Democratic People's Republic of Korea (North Korea) was founded on

Kim Jong-il, leader of North Korea since 1994.

September 9, 1948, under Kim Il-sung, who ruled the communist state until he died in July 1994. In 2008, South Korea had a population of about 48.5 million and North Korea had 23.5 million. Over a million Korean soldiers remain deployed against each other along the world's most heavily fortified border separating the North and the South.

The DPRK originally had a larger industrial base than the ROK. It has a socialist economy, with the means of production largely in the hands of the government. Since the death of Kim Il-sung in 1994, his son, Kim Jong-il, has ruled North Korea. While the country still largely follows the policy of *juche* (self-reliance), the younger Kim seems more interested in modernizing his country and seeking diplomatic relations with the United States and Japan. He has proposed a new development strategy of building *kangsong taeguk* (強盛大國 a strong and prosperous great state), which is similar to the Japanese objective before World War II and the declared objectives of South Korean leader Park Chung-hee in the 1970s. Japan had adopted the strategy of *fukoku kyohei* (富国強兵 enriching the country, strengthening the military) during the Meiji Restoration in the 1860s.

In the famines of the 1990s, two to three million North Koreans reportedly starved to death and the country was forced to turn to the international community for food and fuel. Instead of reforms, North Korea had chosen a "military first" strategy in the past few decades. The younger Kim also resorted to nuclear blackmail, which has led to increased international pressure on the North's economy. Despite some progress made since 2003 in the Six-Party talks (China, the United States, Russia, Japan, and the two Koreas are participants), which aim to terminate North Korea's nuclear program, the nuclear issue remains a major obstacle in relations between North Korea and the United States and Japan.

After touring China and seeing the fruits of its economic reforms, Kim Jong-il began to initiate hesitant reform measures in 2002. The Rajin-Sŏnbong Special Economic Zone was set up in the mid-1990s to attract foreign direct investment (FDI), much like the special economic zones (SEZs) in the PRC.

Korean women and children search the rubble of Seoul for anything that can be used or burned as fuel. November 1, 1950. Capt. F. L. Scheiber. (Army)

The Rajin-Sŏnbong region was split from North Hamgyŏng Province in 1993 under the name "Rajin-Sŏnbong" (shortened to "Rasŏn" 罗先 in 2000). Joint ventures with the South were established. For example, Unification of Korean Technologies (UNIKOTECH), a joint venture to develop and produce a simultaneous translation system over mobile phones, was set up in 2000. A North-South joint auto firm, Peace Motors, was also established in 2000. In addition, the Mount Kumgang tourism project was launched in 1998 to enable South Koreans to cross the border and visit the North.

Unlike the North, South Korea lacks natural resources. The small infrastructure base built during Japanese rule was mostly destroyed during the Korean War. As late as the 1960s, very few people in the world thought South Korea could pull itself out of poverty. Per capita income in the early 1960s was even lower than those of Haiti, Ethiopia, and Yemen and about 40 percent below India's.[1] Unemployment and poverty were widespread with over 40 percent of the nation's population suffering from absolute poverty. Given these circumstances, South Korea's "rags to riches" story is not just fascinating but truly miraculous.

South Korea has grown from a poor developing country to a wealthy developed country. From the mid to late twentieth century, it enjoyed exponential economic growth, with one of the fastest growth rates in modern world history. The nation's GDP per capita grew from only $100 in 1963 to a record-breaking $10,000 in 1995 and $27,100 in 2008. This phenomenon has been referred to as the "miracle on the Han River." Running through the capital city of Seoul, the Han River and its surrounding area has played a significant role in Korean history and economic growth. In comparison, North Korea's GDP per capita in 2008 was about $1,800 (adjusted for PPP).

The post–Korean War develop-ment strategy in South Korea can be divided into three phases: import substitution (1954–60), export orientation (1961–79), and balance and stabilization (post-1980). Import substitution industrialization is a trade and economic policy based on the premise that a country can reduce its foreign dependence through the local production of industrialized products. It was adopted by many Latin American countries from the 1930s to the late 1980s and by some Asian and African countries from the 1950s on. Import substitution policies in the wake of the Korean War resulted in lackluster growth performance, with an average real annual growth rate of 3.4 percent between 1953 and 1960. This period, however, was devoted to building the physical and human capital infrastructure that served as the basis for subsequent industrial development.

The second phase, export-oriented industrialization, began with President

Park Chung-hee, South Korean leader from 1961 to 1979, was credited with South Korea's economic growth in the 1960s and 1970s, but he was also criticized for his authoritarian rule.

Park Chung-hee's military regime in 1961. For the next twenty years, the state-guided, export-based strategy of industrialization worked successfully. Export-oriented industrialization aims to speed up the industrialization process in a country through the exportation of goods for which the nation has a comparative advantage. The success of the "Asian tigers"—Hong Kong, South Korea, Taiwan, and Singapore—in the post–World War II period is often credited to this strategy. Between 1962 and 1979, South Korea's real GNP and exports grew at average annual rates of 9.3 and 33.7 percent, respectively. Leading ROK exports included electronics, textiles and footwear, automobiles and automobile parts, shipbuilding materials, and chemicals.

By the end of the 1970s, however, the Korean economy had overextended itself, and structural imbalances and bottlenecks were beginning to manifest themselves. The high growth rate led to a rapid buildup of foreign debt and inflation, with widening disparities within industry as well as between rural and urban areas. The assassination of President Park in 1979, the oil-induced worldwide economic recession in 1980–81, and domestic crop failures compelled the new government to impose stabilization programs. The government started removing subsidies and preferential loans and called for an efficient allocation of investment to allow domestic industries to develop more in line with the shifting comparative advantages

Syngman Rhee, the first president of South Korea after it was founded in 1948, led his country through the Korean War.

in the global market. South Korea also participated militarily in the Vietnam War in the late 1960s and the early 1970s and provided war-related supplies to the American troops, resulting in substantial foreign exchange earnings.

South Korea's industrialization did not take place at the expense of other sectors, notably agriculture. There were periods, particularly the early 1970s, when agriculture came to the fore of the development strategy, and the South Korean government was able to avoid an excessive urban-rural income disparity. The government did not have to spend a large percentage of its budget on social welfare and could concentrate its limited resources on high-growth sectors of the economy.

In 1996, South Korea became a member of the OECD, a milestone in its development history. Its economy slowly rebounded after the 1997 Asian financial crisis. Its average growth rate for the 1991–95 period was 7.5 percent, but it slipped to 4.6 percent in 2001–07 following the crisis. In 2008, South Korea's economy was the third largest in Asia after Japan and China and the thirteenth largest in the world in total GNP.

CHAEBOL

The *chaebol*, a form of business conglomerate, is the symbol of South Korea's economic success. Several dozen such large, family-controlled, government-assisted corporate groups have played a major role in the South Korean economy since the 1960s. Some have become well-known international brand names such as Samsung, Hyundai, and LG. The *chaebol* are powerful independent actors in the economy and politics, and they cooperate with the government in planning and innovation. The government has worked hard to encourage competition among them in sectors such as the electronics and auto industries to avoid monopoly.

Chaebol and their leaders helped pull the Korean economy out of poverty and eventually made it globally competitive. Lee Byung-Chul, founder of the Samsung Group, started a small trading company with forty employees in 1938. In 1953, he opened a sugar refinery, South Korea's first manufacturing facility after the Korean War. The company prospered under Lee's philosophy of making Samsung the leader in each industry he entered. After his initial success, he ventured into service businesses such as insurance, securities, and department stores in the 1960s and 1970s. South Korean President Park Chung-hee's regime helped Samsung and many other Korean firms. President Park placed great importance on economic growth and development, and he assisted large, profitable companies, protecting them from competition and aiding them financially as well. His government banned several foreign companies that were selling consumer electronics in South Korea. This helped Samsung enormously when it began to manufacture the first Korean dynamic random access memory chips. As it continued to thrive in the domestic market, Samsung invested heavily in research and development and began to go global in the late 1980s and early 1990s, turning the company into a worldwide leader in the electronics industry. In 1982, it built a television assembly plant in Portugal; in 1984, it built a $25 million plant in New York; and in 1987 it built another $25 million facility in England.

Chaebol are often compared to Japan's *keiretsu*, the successors to the prewar *zaibatsu* (in fact, *chaebol* and *zaibatsu* are Korean and Japanese pronunciations of the same Chinese characters, 財閥). While *chaebol* are similar to *keiretsu*, there are many differences between them (see Table 3.1).

DEMOCRACY AND DEVELOPMENT

South Korea's transformation from a poor, authoritarian state to a prosperous, democratic one raises an interesting question: can or should a country focus on economic modernization before political democratization? An important issue in international political economy is how economic development and political regimes interact. The political scientist Seymour Martin Lipset pointed out in the 1950s that a high level of economic development makes democracy more likely. Another political scientist, Samuel Huntington, observed that while

Table 3.1. *Chaebol and Keiretsu Compared*

	Chaebol 财阀	Keiretsu 系列
History	Relatively short	Much longer
Management	Largely by founding families	Mostly by professional executives
Ownership	Centralized	More decentralized
Production Structure	Subsidiaries produce components for export products	External contractors are hired for production
Financial Structure	Subject to government regulation in credit allocation. Prohibited from owning private banks	Historically working with an affiliated bank with almost unlimited access to credit

developed countries tend to have stable democracies the process of economic development may lead to political instability, which makes it likely and even desirable to have an authoritarian government during the transition period.[2] South Korea's experience supports both arguments.

After the "people power" movement of 1987 against the heavy-handed governance of President Chun Doo-hwan, the government agreed to a democratic transition based on a pact among elements of the military regime and the two major opposition parties. The 1987 new constitution provided for a democratically elected president limited to one five-year term. All three major protagonists in 1987, Kim Yong-sam, Kim Dae-jung, and Roh Moo-hyun, held presidential office later on. Democracy has been fully consolidated: the military is under control, elections are vigorously contested, and the courts have become major sites for the constraint of politics.

Lee Myung-bak, who became the ROK's seventeenth president in February 2008, was an executive and later president of Hyundai—one of the largest *chaebol*—before he entered politics in 1992. Nicknamed "the Bulldozer," Lee

Kim Dae-jung, the first leader from the South to cross the border to visit North Korea in 2000. Kim won the Nobel Peace Prize in 2000.

was a no-nonsense executive single-mindedly focused on growth. He later paid more attention to quality of life and the environment. In 2005, as mayor of Seoul, he restored a paved-over, four-mile stream in downtown Seoul over which an ugly highway had been built during the "growth at all cost" 1970s. Promising to improve the quality of life for Seoul residents, he had the traffic-clogged elevated highway ripped out and restored the Cheonggyecheon (literally, "clear water stream"), which had been covered over. The project propelled him into the international spotlight, and *Time* magazine named him one of its Heroes of the Environment in 2007.

President Lee wanted to be the chief executive officer of the nation. His stated goals were expressed in "the 747 plan" during his election campaign (a reference to the Boeing 747 aircraft): achieving 7 percent annual growth and $40,000 per capita GDP and making Korea the world's seventh-largest economy. At the beginning of his presidency, South Korea was not among the ten largest economies and had a GDP per capita of about $27,100 (as estimated by the U.S. Central Intelligence Agency in 2008). His rivals argued that the plan was unrealistic and too costly. Others were concerned about possible negative environmental effects.

THE LIMITS OF THE "DEVELOPMENTAL STATE" MODEL

South Korea also followed the developmental state model, with active government guidance of economic activities. While this model has yielded some good economic performances for East Asian economies, it has been blamed by some for the 1997 financial crisis. South Korea had been building great conglomerates to compete on the world stage. The *chaebol*, supported and sometimes controlled by the government, absorbed more and more capital investment. Eventually, excess debt led to major failures and takeovers. The banking sector was burdened with nonperforming loans as large corporations were funding aggressive expansions. In July 1997, South Korea's third-largest car maker, Kia Motors, applied for emergency loans. In 1998, Hyundai took over Kia Motors. The Seoul stock exchange fell by 4 percent on November 7, 1997. On November 8, it plunged by 7 percent, its biggest one-day drop to date. The Korean won, meanwhile, weakened to more than seventeen hundred per dollar from around eight hundred.

As a later developer than Japan, South Korea needed a stronger government to promote economic growth. The South Korean state was even more interventionist than the Japanese. The objective of fast industrialization and the effort to support large businesses were mutually reinforcing. The big South Korean *chaebol* such as Hyundai and Daewoo, which the government

A Buddhist statue gazing at the cityscape of modern Seoul, capital of South Korea.

supported, did become internationally competitive. But cozy state-business relationships sometimes lead to corruption, and that is what happened in South Korea and Japan, hence the name "crony capitalism."[3]

On the other hand, if the state misallocates resources, as in the case of North Korea, where the military receives priority in the distribution of limited resources, economic growth will stagnate and ordinary citizens will remain in poverty.

The term *strong government* has been criticized as implying a compliant society, which is often not the case in East Asia. Even in South Korea, which is often recognized as having the strongest development state in East Asia, the society has sometimes been militantly opposed to the state.[4] The society's power *vis-à-vis* the state was typified by the Gwangju uprising. This popular uprising took place in the city of Gwangju in May 1980 when citizens rose up against Chun Doo-hwan's military dictatorship. The uprising was crushed by the South Korean military with hundreds of civilian casualties, but it helped to pave the way for South Korean democratization.

Since the early 1990s, South Korean farmers' protests against globalization and free trade have captured global attention. In 2007 and 2008, consumers and farmers demonstrated against the US-ROK Free Trade Agreement, especially U.S. beef exports to South Korea. Such antiglobalization movements are also found in Taiwan, Japan, and China.

4

THE PRC AND TAIWAN: THE STORY OF A "DRAGON" AND A "TIGER"

China's phenomenal economic transformation and achievements since the late 1970s raise a few interesting questions. How does its development path differ from those of other East Asian economies? Is China moving toward democracy? And what are the main development challenges for China's future?

Modern Chinese history began with the so-called "century of humiliation." China suffered enormously as a result of clashes with the Western powers in the nineteenth century. The "century of humiliation" began in 1839 when the British used "gunboat diplomacy" to impose unfair trade practices on the Qing dynasty. When the Chinese resisted, the British started the Opium War, which lasted from 1839 to 1842, weakened the Qing dynasty, and marked the beginning of the colonization and exploitation of China. France, the United States, Russia, Germany, and later Japan all took advantage of China's weakness to establish spheres of influence. They forced the Qing to sign unequal treaties recognizing their zones of incursion. It was during this period that the British forced China to cede Hong Kong to them as a colony, and Japan took Taiwan as a colony after it defeated China in the first Sino-Japanese War (1894–95). After Chinese revolutionaries overthrew the Qing dynasty in 1911, the country suffered internal strife for nearly four decades due to warlordism, civil war, and the Japanese invasion.

Revolutionaries such as Dr. Sun Yat-sen attempted to save China by introducing "Mr. Science" and "Mr. Democracy." Sun and his followers established the Republic of China (ROC) in 1911 after the dynasty collapsed. The Republic's founding father proposed "three principles of the people" (三民主义)—the principle of *Minzhu* (Nationalism), the principle of *Minquan* (People's Power), and the principle of *Minsheng* (People's Livelihood)—to save the beleaguered nation. Sun's "three principles" were apparently inspired by "government of the people, by the people, and for the people," the phrase Abraham Lincoln used in the Gettysburg Address. Unfortunately, competition for power by warlords and Sun's death in 1925 dashed the hope for a democratic China.

The Chinese Civil War of the 1940s eventually created "two Chinas." Chiang Kai-shek and his Nationalist forces were defeated on the mainland and retreated to the island of Taiwan off the southeast coast. The Republic of China government, though beaten on the battlefield, was not destroyed; instead, it survived and prospered in Taiwan. On the mainland, Mao Zedong's Communist forces unified most of the country and established the People's Republic of China in October 1949. The "century of humiliation" ended with Mao's powerful declaration at Tiananmen Square that all foreign influences had been driven out of China and "the Chinese people have stood up." The two Chinese governments took different development paths. Sixty years later, Taiwan, one of the four "little dragons," is free and prosperous and the PRC, after three decades of ultraleftist policies, is quickly modernizing and building a market economy with Chinese characteristics.

The Chinese Communists made many social and political changes, starting in the 1950s with the transition to a planned economy. Mao also launched a series of political campaigns, including the "Great Leap Forward" (1958–61), during which he boasted that China would catch up with Great Britain and the United States in industrialization within fifteen years. As a result of this unrealistic, radical policy, millions of Chinese starved to death. Mao later orchestrated the "Cultural Revolution" (1966–76), during which young cadres were encouraged to "make revolution" and attack intellectuals and veteran party leaders. During this decade, colleges across China were closed and economic growth lagged even farther behind that of its thriving neighbors. In the first three decades of PRC history, the country had only limited trade with the Soviet Union and a few developing nations. It was essentially isolated from the Western world and the global economy. Shortly after Mao's death in 1976, the Chinese government, under Deng Xiaoping's leadership, introduced economic reforms as well as limited political reforms and began to open itself to the West again.

THE TAIWANESE "MIRACLE"

When the ROC government recovered Taiwan from its Japanese colonizers in 1945, the island was in a state of widespread destruction. Railways, roads, and harbors were basically operating at half capacity. Outbound transportation was inconvenient and manufacturing productivity sharply reduced. Basic necessities were in short supply, and prices were continuously skyrocketing.

When Chiang Kai-shek and his Kuomintang (KMT) government fled to Taiwan in 1949 following the Chinese Civil War, they brought China's precious metals and foreign currency reserves to the island with them. Many mainland business and intellectual elites also escaped to Taiwan.

The KMT government took advantage of the still-functioning agricultural and industrial infra-structure built by the Japanese as well as what raw materials and food reserves remained on the island. It also instituted several laws and land reforms that had never been effectively enacted on the mainland. Some of these reforms are briefly described later in this chapter.

Chiang Kai-shek, a nationalist who strongly believed in "one China."

Huge amounts of American aid also injected new blood into Taiwan's economic life. The United States provided short-term financial assistance, easy credit, and military support, which helped Taiwan raise the necessary capital to restart its economy. The United States then temporarily terminated aid to Taiwan after the PRC was established in 1949. After the Korean War broke out in 1950, the U.S. government resumed its economic aid and assisted in the defense of the Taiwan Strait as part of the Cold War. This not only boosted morale but also stabilized the island's economy.

The KMT government was determined to develop Taiwan into a solid base for its efforts to "recover" the lost Chinese mainland. Chiang Kai-shek initially hoped to return to the mainland but gradually accepted the fact that the ROC government was in Taiwan to stay. While maintaining its military preparedness, Taiwan quickly adopted land and other economic reforms.

Sun Yat-sen had made "land to the tiller" a foundation of the early Chinese republic, but the KMT never had sufficient control over China to implement any reforms. In the 1950s, Taiwan's land reform and community development plans were carried out by the Sino-American Joint Commission on Rural Reconstruction (JCRR). The JCRR was established in 1948, before the move to Taiwan, and funded by U.S. Congress based on a provision in the China Aid Act of 1948. It was led by five commissioners, three of whom were Chinese, appointed by the Chinese government, and two of whom were

American, appointed by the American President. In 1949, with the impending defeat of the KMT and its retreat to Taiwan, the JCRR moved to the island, where under the leadership of Chiang Monlin (Jiang Menglin) it supervised major land reforms, agricultural improvements, and education projects. The Columbia-educated Chiang had previously served as the President of Peking (Beijing) University and Zhejiang University and as the Minister of Education under the ROC government.

Many of the large landowners in Taiwan were Japanese who had fled. Those who stayed were compensated with commercial and industrial properties seized after Taiwan reverted from Japanese rule in 1945. Starting in 1949, rents were reduced to 37.5 percent of the original and landlords were required to provide six-year leases. Tenants were no longer required to pay rent in advance, and during times of crop failure they could apply for a reduction. This had the immediate effect of lowering land prices and facilitating the process of land redistribution. The KMT government also sold public lands abandoned by the Japanese to farmers at a fixed rate. The farmer was loaned the money and could repay it in kind over ten years. Later, larger landowners were forced to sell their land, except for small amounts, on the same terms. The land program succeeded in part because the KMT had come from the mainland and had few ties to the local landowners. Like the 1947 land reform in Japan, it created small independent farmers whose economic resources were enhanced by their new status.

To accomplish the central mission of economic growth, the Taiwanese government allowed technocrats rather than politicians to handle economic decision making. Since Taiwanese natives controlled the private sector, the government created state-owned enterprises to promote heavy industrialization. It was also easier for an outsider government without local ties to conduct these reforms, which not only benefited the economy but also benefited the KMT by weakening local power bases that might have posed a challenge to its rule. At the same time, the KMT allowed Taiwanese businesses to operate with few restrictions, limiting the scope of the state enterprises. There was thus plenty of room for social mobility and economic advancement.[1]

Individual businesses and corporate entrepreneurs played an essential role in helping make Taiwan one of the most dynamic and globally competitive economies in the world. One of them, Wang Yung-ching (also known as Y.C. Wang 王永庆), founded a large business empire. He served as chairman of the board of the Formosa Plastics Corporation, one of the largest plastics manufacturers in the world, until June 2006, when he stepped down at the age of eighty-nine. He also chaired the boards of the Nan Ya Plastics

A night view of Taipei with the Taipei 101 Tower (October 2006). As of early 2009, the 101-floor Taipei landmark remained the world's tallest skyscraper. © Imaginechina.

Corporation, the Formosa Chemistry and Fibre Corporation, and the Cyma Plywood and Lumber Company. His businesses funded Taiwan's Ming-chi Institute of Technology, Chang Gung Memorial Hospital, and Chang Gung University. His global investments have focused on the United States and mainland China. Several of his children followed in his footsteps and became well established in the semiconductor, computer, and other industries. Wang died in his sleep at age 91 in October 2008 during a visit to the U.S.

Prior to 1962, Taiwan's agricultural production contributed more to GDP than industrial production; in 1952, agriculture's share of GDP was 32.2 percent and that of industry 16.7 percent. However, in 1961 agriculture's share fell to just 25 percent, while the industrial sector's share rose to 23.7 percent. In 1962, the value of industrial production began to exceed that of agriculture, and this period is generally referred to as Taiwan's "industrial era." By 1986, industrial output had climbed to a full 47.1 percent of GDP. Between 1952 and 1982, economic growth averaged 8.7 percent, and GDP grew by 360 percent between 1965 and 1986. The period between 1963 and 1980 witnessed the most rapid growth in the history of Taiwan. Despite the adverse effects of two energy crises, it maintained an annual growth rate of 10 percent. The income gap between rich and poor declined during this period. The Gini coefficient—an internationally applied index that measures income inequality—was 0.558 in 1953 and fell to 0.303 in 1980, a score even lower than those of some Western European countries.[2] Health care, education, and quality of life also greatly improved during this period.

Taiwan's economy has been boosted by its robust exports, and as of 2008 it has the world's fifth-largest foreign exchange reserves after the PRC, Japan, Russia, and India. It is the world's largest supplier of computer chips and a leading liquid crystal display (LCD) panel and networking equipment manufacturer and consumer electronics designer and manufacturer. Textile production is another major industrial export sector, although its importance has declined due to fierce competition from other economies.

THE UNITED STATES AND THE "TWO CHINAS"

Recognizing that Chiang Kai-shek could never defend Taiwan against Mao's powerful and still growing forces, the United States was prepared to abandon it in the late 1940s. To a great extent, the Korean War saved Taiwan. Shortly after the war broke out, the United States sent its Seventh Fleet into the Taiwan Strait, forestalling an imminent PRC attack on the island. The signing of the US-ROC (Taiwan) Mutual Defense Treaty in 1954 officially put Taiwan under U.S. military protection.

The Korean War made the PRC and the United States, which had been exploring mutual diplomatic recognition, into enemies. Although official contacts continued in places such as Warsaw, relations did not improve until President Richard Nixon's 1972 visit to China. A year earlier the United Nations had recognized the PRC rather than the ROC as China's legitimate government. In 1973, the United States established a liaison office in Beijing, with George H. W. Bush serving as its head in 1974 and 1975. In 1979, the United States and the PRC finally established diplomatic relations and Washington cut its official ties with Taiwan. In a joint communiqué, the United States acknowledged that Taiwan was part of China and that the PRC was the sole government representing it.

Years later many in Taiwan still cannot forgive the United States for its "betrayal," and President Jimmy Carter, who normalized diplomatic ties with Beijing, is still verbally attacked by some politicians. However, it was President Carter who also signed the "Taiwan Relations Act" (TRA) into law in April 1979, the statute that has regulated the U.S.-Taiwan unofficial relationship ever since. These relations are sometimes described as "officially unofficial and unofficially official." Although neither the PRC nor Taiwan is completely satisfied with the arrangement, many argue that the dual U.S. approach (i.e., officially recognizing the PRC while maintaining strong nongovernmental relations with Taiwan) serves the best interests of the United States. Under this framework, the United States has continued to provide weapons to Taiwan for defensive purposes and, perhaps most significantly, Taiwan has prospered and democratized.

Taiwan's democratization was gradual and peaceful. In the 1950s and 1960s, it suffered under the so-called white terror, during which over 140,000 people were jailed or executed for opposing KMT rule. In 1986, President Chiang Ching-kuo, Chiang Kai-shek's son, initiated democratic reforms by expanding political participation, and the opposition Democratic Progressive Party (DPP) was

Chiang Ching-kuo, Chiang Kai-shek's son, introduced democratic reforms in Taiwan in the 1980s.

formed. Martial law, which had been imposed in May 1949, was finally lifted in July 1987. The younger Chiang was hoping that a democratic Taiwan would serve as a vanguard for democratizing mainland China. In Taiwan's first democratic presidential election in 1996, Lee Teng-hui, the KMT chairman but also an advocate of Taiwan independence, was elected to a four-year term. In 2000, the opposition DPP leader Chen Shui-bian won the presidential election in a peaceful transition of power. In 2004, Chen was reelected in a hotly contested race after he suffered two mysterious bullet wounds on election eve. The KMT and many others allege that Chen staged the assassination attempt in order to win a sympathy vote, a strategy that apparently succeeded.

After eight years of lackluster rule by the DPP, Taiwan's economy, which was also affected by the global economic fluctuations, was much weakened, and so was its international position. The number of countries that recognize Taiwan had dropped from thirty-one to twenty-three by 2008. President Chen repeatedly claimed that China and Taiwan were two separate countries on each side of the Taiwan Strait. Some people in Taiwan are also experiencing an identity crisis. The majority used to consider themselves as both Taiwanese and Chinese, but now many people identify themselves as Taiwanese only as a result of the Chen administration's desinicization policy, a policy designed to deliberately cut Taiwan's links to China and make it a separate country. Cross-Strait relations were extremely tense during Chen's tenure, and Beijing adopted a strategy of waiting Chen out. Chen was arrested and indicted for forgery, money-laundering, and misuse of public funds at the end of 2008.

Since the victory of KMT leader Ma Ying-jeou in the March 2008 presidential elections, Taiwan has adopted a more moderate policy toward mainland China, and cross-Strait relations have greatly improved. Mainland Chinese can now visit Taiwan. In December 2008, direct passenger flights, shipping, and postal services across the Taiwan Strait were reinstated for the first time in nearly six decades. Many restrictions on Taiwanese investment on the mainland imposed by previous Taiwanese administrations have been lifted.

THE CHINESE "MIRACLE"

On the mainland, Mao Zedong's often turbulent role plunged China into deep social, economic, cultural, and political chaos, and in 1976, at the end of the Cultural Revolution, the Chinese economy was on the brink of collapse. Deng Xiaoping, the next significant PRC leader, initiated pragmatic and experimental policies that fundamentally changed the fate of China. His "cat theory," which claims that it doesn't matter whether a cat is white or black so long as it catches mice, put an end to the ideological debate between socialism and capitalism in China. Officially, beginning with Deng, the PRC has been building "socialism with Chinese characteristics." A closer look at China's policies and practices in the past three decades suggests that the PRC is probably building "capitalism with Chinese characteristics."

Some suggest that China has adopted an economic system of state capitalism, although the political structure is still under the tight control of the Communist Party. Deng's vision notwithstanding, what other factors have helped propel China's economic growth? What is unique about China's experience? Can Taiwan, as a Chinese society, serve as a beacon for the mainland's continued pursuit of modernization and democracy?

China's reforms began in the late 1970s in the countryside, where Deng introduced the "household responsibility system," under which farmers could rent a piece of land from the state and sell their

Mao Zedong and his Communist forces defeated Chiang Kai-shek's Nationalists and founded the People's Republic of China in 1949. China under Mao was one of the poorest nations in the world.

Shenzhen city in south China's Guangdong province. After being designated as a Special Economic Zone in 1979, Shenzhen quickly transformed from a small fishing village into a large metropolis. Photo © Imaginechina

surplus crops on the open market. Rural entrepreneurs were also encouraged to establish their own businesses, called "township and village enterprises."

Meanwhile, China reopened trade with the West. At first, its strategy was *yin jin lai*, which means "to bring in" foreign direct investment. In 1979 the PRC established four special economic zones (SEZs) in southern China near Hong Kong, Taiwan, and Southeast Asia to attract direct investment from overseas Chinese and Western businesses. Investors enjoyed preferential treatment in taxation and exports. China was very cautious in this initiative since these were new reform policies. With the SEZ experiment, China was "crossing the river while groping for the stone," as Deng Xiaoping put it. The SEZs turned out to be a great success. For example, Shenzhen, the best-known SEZ, grew literally overnight from a small fishing village into a glitzy modern metropolis.

After the success of the SEZs, Deng opened up the whole coastal area, including Shanghai, in the late 1980s and early 1990s. In his famous 1992 "southern tour," he praised what the SEZs especially Shenzhen had achieved and urged the rest of China to "move faster and be bolder." He did not include Shanghai in the first wave of economic liberalization in the early 1980s, fearing that if the Shanghai experiment failed the whole nation's economy would suffer seriously since Shanghai alone accounted for one-sixth of the national GDP. Shanghai began to prosper later, in the early 1990s when its modern Pudong district emerged on the east side of the Huangpu River. In the twenty-first century, Shanghai remains China's economic and commercial center.

After over two decades of *yin jin lai*, China adopted a new strategy, *zou chu qu* or "going out," in the late 1990s. Chinese companies began to invest abroad, just as Japanese companies had a couple of decades before. As an example of *zou chu qu*, in the summer of 2005 the China National Offshore Oil Company, Ltd. (CNOOC), attempted to purchase Unocal, a small California oil company, although the sale was aborted due to political pressure from the U.S. Congress. China has invested heavily in Africa, Latin America, the Middle East, and Central Asia, especially in energy sectors. In November 2007, the Industrial and Commercial Bank of China announced that it would be purchasing a 20 percent stake in the Standard Bank of South Africa worth $5.6 billion.

The PRC's GDP has been growing by an average of 10 percent a year for thirty years since economic reform began, and industrial production is galloping ahead at an annual rate of 17 percent. China's 2001 admission into the World Trade Organization has only served to accelerate that growth. The World Bank now estimates that exports represent a quarter of China's GDP, five times the level of 1978. By 2007, China's economy was the third-largest in the world, behind the United States and Japan, and there are predictions that it may assume the top spot as early as 2025. Based on purchasing power parity (PPP)—a calculation that equalizes the purchasing power of different currencies in their home countries for a given basket of goods—China already has the world's second-largest economy, although in per capita terms it is still in the lower-middle-income bracket. The restructuring of the economy and resulting efficiency gains have contributed to a more than tenfold increase in GDP since 1978. China has succeeded in lifting 250 million people out of abject poverty since the reforms began. Per capita GDP (based on PPP) was estimated at $6,100 in 2008, a huge jump from just a few hundred dollars twenty years ago.

The "miracle" comes with a heavy price. While living standards have improved for most people and a growing number of Chinese are getting rich, the income gap between rich and poor is widening, as is the gap between

The Shanghai Skyline at Night—the Oriental Pearl TV Tower (tallest left), Jinmao Tower (tallest second right) and the Shanghai World Financial Center (tallest right) in Lujiazui Financial District in Pudong, Shanghai, China, July 2008. Shanghai currently remains China's economic and commercial center. Photo © Imaginechina.

urban and rural areas. In China, the Gini coefficient has reached over 0.45, indicating a very uneven distribution of income. In addition, much of China's natural environment has been destroyed in the process of fast economic growth.

China's market reform was incremental, unlike Soviet-style of "shock therapy." China's transformation was pragmatic and based on local conditions since Deng Xiaoping was trying to build "socialism with Chinese characteristics." Different from the Soviet Union's political and economic reforms under Mikhail Gorbachev's *perestroika* (economic restructuring) and *glasnost* (political openness) programs, Deng's economic reform adopted a step-by-step approach. The scope and pace of liberalization were carefully controlled and sometimes halted by conservatives in the party. Economic liberalization was first implemented and tested in a few provinces or special economic zones. Only after these regions were successful were reform measures introduced and developed in the rest of the country.

The process of industrialization and structural change in China has been part of a general economic transition from a centrally planned to a market economy. Policy support has consisted of gradual and selective adoption of regulations in accordance with the appropriate pace and pattern of the transition. Key elements have been a reduction of the role of state-owned enterprises (SOEs); the gradual and selective introduction of market incentives through the regulatory reform of price systems; and government control of domestic labor mobility, external trade, and FDI. Government policy has also played an important role in directing both domestic and foreign investment toward specific sectors such as the manufacture of consumer products.

Fixed investment that benefited from preferential credit, mainly from state-owned banks, grew very quickly between the late 1980s and the late 1990s and was directed at targeted industries and sectors. Moreover, manufacturing industries enjoyed tax incentives more favorable than those imposed on other industries. The economy has also been heavily influenced by sizable public investment in physical infrastructure, direct government financing, the provision of credit at preferential interest rates, and tax rebates. In the absence of an efficient domestic securities market, bank loans have been the major source of corporate finance.

The Chinese government has influenced the sectoral distribution of FDI inflows. Guidelines and regulations were issued whereby FDI inflows were categorized as "prohibited," "permitted," or "encouraged." In the encouraged type, such as high-tech industries, incentives were given through extensive policies of preferential treatment such as tax rebates and/or exemptions, duty-free imports of capital equipment, and better access to public infrastructure and utilities. Administrative procedures were also streamlined for "free trade and high-technology development zones," and incentive packages were provided, including heavily subsidized land and energy provisions.

Prior to its accession to the WTO, China's trade policy was very industry selective, with extensive import restrictions, in order to support industrial restructuring. First, gradual and phased trade liberalization enabled imports of technology that China would not otherwise have had access to and were essential to making structural changes in Chinese industry. Second, foreign trade allowed the exportation of surplus production without which these structural changes, based on a combination of a large surplus of labor and rapidly increasing investment, would not have been sustainable. Exporting firms benefited from various pricing, tax, and loan privileges, as well as support for technological upgrades.

With the deepening of its economic reforms and, in particular, the decentralization of foreign trade, which has led to a massive entrance of private enterprises, many of the incentives have been phased out, nontariff barriers have been gradually dismantled, and tariff barriers have been significantly lowered.[3]

Privatization was gradual and even controversial in China. But by the first decade of the new century the percentage of the national economy directly controlled by the state sector had declined to about one-third. Private ownership was legalized when the Property Law of the People's Republic of China was adopted by the National People's Congress, China's nominal legislative body, and went into effect on October 1, 2007.

The law is a milestone on the path toward a market economy. The legislation stopped short of abrogating the principle that all land belongs to the state, a fundamental part of the communist system put in place after Mao Zedong's rise to power in 1949. But it broke ground by establishing new protections for private homes and businesses and for farmers with long-term leases on their fields. These goals had long been sought by the entrepreneurs who now account for more than half of China's production, by the swiftly climbing number of urban families that have bought their own apartments, and by the millions of farmers whose croplands have come under growing pressure from real estate developers.

One of the keys to success in China's economic reform has been the willingness to experiment, to try different approaches to solving common problems and then evaluate the results free of political dogma. Deng Xiaoping's pragmatic policies were essential in China's transition from a tightly controlled planned economy to the largely market economy of today.

THE BEIJING CONSENSUS?

Neither coined nor sanctioned by the Chinese government, the term *Beijing Consensus* has gained popularity in recent years. It was first suggested by Joshua Cooper Ramo, a journalist-editor, to summarize the developmental model based on economic liberalization under tight political control.

Does the Chinese model represent something vastly different from the Japanese or Korean model? Does it challenge the *Washington Consensus*, which suggests that the best way to achieve economic growth is through the adoption of a series of liberal, free-market, economic and political policies? Whether the *Beijing Consensus* challenges the *Washington Consensus* or not remains a policy debate, but already some developing countries in Africa and Latin America seem very interested in this Chinese development path.

Deng Xiaoping is often compared to Mikhail Gorbachev as both were creative leaders who tried to reform a communist system. Gorbachev introduced *glasnost* (political openness) and *perestroika* (economic restructuring) simultaneously, reform policies that unleashed forces leading to the demise of the Soviet Union. In contrast, Deng believed it was important to maintain the party's dominance, which was crucial for creating a stable social environment for economic development. By choosing to start with economic reform and introducing it so very cautiously, the Chinese Communist Party had a greater capacity to manage the change, and China's economy prospered without fundamentally changing the country's political structure. But is such a strategy sustainable?

Much of the Washington consensus was right, especially the points that focused on sound macroeconomic policies such as fiscal discipline and public expenditures on health care, education, and infrastructure. Indeed, China itself has followed some of these macroeconomic policies. Clearly, one should not look at China's experience from the dichotomy of the *Beijing Consensus* versus *Washington Consensus*. China's development, with its different political and economic approaches, is more complicated than a single model can describe.

MAJOR DEVELOPMENT CHALLENGES AHEAD

The speed of China's progression from a low-income, populous country to a global economic force has continued to astound many analysts and observers. Academics and policymakers in the developed and developing world continue to examine China's progress and its impact on regional and world economies.

A growing China has growing pains. Its prosperous surface masks a rising sea of problems and challenges. China's economic achievements since the late 1970s have made its development experience distinct in many ways from those of many other economies. Its robust economic growth, which has brought the country to the status of one of the largest economies in the world, has dramatically reduced poverty. However, analysts in China are still grappling with various questions: How can this rapid economic growth be sustained? What can be done to close the remaining gap between China and the world's leading economies as quickly as possible? How can welfare benefits for its population be further enhanced? How can environmental challenges be addressed? How will China move from a reliance on labor-intensive, cheap goods to developing its brand names based on high technology, as did Japan, South Korea, and Taiwan?

Behind the dazzling skylines and impressive statistics, another reality exists in China, one replete with unresolved problems and daunting numbers that suggest a far darker scenario. For example, China must create some 12 to 15 million new jobs annually just to keep up with population growth;

the government must deal with an estimated 270 million unemployed or underemployed people; and a "floating population" (rural workers who have moved to the cities to find work) of about 150 million, the largest migration in human history, is growing by almost 5 percent annually. These migrants have no job security, no long-term housing, and no health care; China has no functioning pension system, and the cost of creating one is estimated to be in the hundreds of billions of dollars.[4] On the other hand, a new middle class eager to protect its newfound property rights and quality of life is beginning to challenge government policies. Health, environment, and labor activists around the country are agitating to force the authorities to respect laws and citizens' rights.

While China has overcome many difficulties in the process of rapid economic growth, the country is still faced with many problems. Some are the unavoidable consequences of the ongoing transition from central planning, while others have emerged in the process of development. Some are strictly domestic, while others involve external relations. Some have not been encountered by other East Asian economies, including greater pressure to comply with international trade rules, to improve human rights, and to democratize. Several major challenges particularly need to be addressed.

How Long Can Political Democracy and Economic Growth Remain Divorced?

One of the biggest challenges for China is to bring the political system more into line with the economic system. Can a "harmonious society," as advocated by President Hu Jintao, be established without political reform? Modernization theories suggest that as a society develops, a rising middle class will serve as the stimulus for a democratic movement. Singapore is an obvious exception, and China could prove these modernization theories wrong again. China's somewhat unique combination of state-led, market-based, economic development and a socialist legacy give most socioeconomic sectors, especially the growing middle class, an interest in maintaining the political status quo since this is the group that benefits the most from the current political and economic structure.

The movement that culminated in the 1989 Tiananmen Square incident, understood in the West as a pro-democracy movement, started in Beijing and other large cities as college students went to the streets to express their frustration over such social problems as rising prices, poor treatment of intellectuals, and rampant corruption. With the booming economy and the loosening of government controls, corruption has grown in a seemingly greater proportion than the economy. Widespread corruption not only threatens to erode the foundation of the Chinese economy but also tarnishes China's and the Communist Party's image.

While the overall economic reforms have been undertaken effectively, financial reform has received a low priority. With bad debts and real estate bubbles, China's fragile financial system may not withstand major economic fluctuations if the global economy slows down in the future. In 2008, as the global economic downturn hit China, Chinese exports dropped for the first time in seven years.

Uneven Development

China is rapidly urbanizing. It is moving from a peasant society to an industrial powerhouse. As late as the 1980s, 80 percent of the population lived in rural areas. By the early twenty-first century, the ratio had dropped to about 60 percent. China is experiencing a growing development gap between coastal and inland and urban and rural areas. Because market-based operations have expanded, inequality in the distribution of income and wealth is likely to increase in the near future. Despite the overall enhancement of standards of living, China is missing social safety nets that could support the most disadvantaged groups in the society.

Class issues have grown as a result of uneven economic development. An underclass of migrant workers—the "floating population"—has developed, not only creating infrastructure challenges to the cities but more seriously perpetuating the division between rich and poor and creating social tensions. These 150 million plus internal migrants who have relocated from rural to urban areas not only are looked down on by urban residents but do not enjoy the same level of social benefits. Their children cannot enroll in urban public schools. As has happened during industrialization worldwide, migration to the cities has also served to break up the traditional family and community structures that have been the basis of much of Chinese culture. China also needs to sustain adequate job growth for tens of millions of workers laid off from state-owned enterprises, migrants, and new entrants to the workforce such as college graduates.

Mass protests have become common in contemporary China. According to its official statistics, in 2004 alone there were 74,000 "mass incidents" (demonstrations and riots), an increase from 58,000 the year before and only 10,000 a decade ago. In addition, a sharp rise in crime rates is eroding the stability of Chinese society. And one demographic consequence of the "family

Palace Museum, Beijing, in heavy smog. According to the World Health Organization (WHO), seventeen of the twenty most polluted cities in the world are located in China. Photo © Imaginechina.

planning" policy is that China is now one of the most rapidly aging countries in the world.

Environmental Degradation

After three decades of rapid economic development, most of China's rivers are black with industrial and human waste. Just two decades ago many of these rivers were clean enough for drinking and swimming. In many Chinese cities, it is hard to see a blue sky even on a sunny day. According to the World Health Organization (WHO), seventeen of the twenty most polluted cities in the world are located in China. China also boasts one-third of the world's cigarette smokers. By early 2008, it had replaced the United States as the world's largest emitter of carbon dioxide, the main greenhouse gas. Despite strenuous efforts, Beijing's air quality was not significantly improved during the 2008 Summer Olympics. Heavy air pollution returned to Beijing shortly after the games.

Deterioration of the environ-ment—most notably air pollution, soil erosion, and a steady fall in the water table, especially in the north—is a long-term problem. China continues to lose arable land because of erosion and economic development. In 2007, the government intensified its efforts to

Soldiers help with rescue efforts after the May 12, 2008 earthquake in Beichuan county, Mianzhu city, southwest China's Sichuan province. The Chinese government was praised by many for the way it quickly mobilized to rescue survivors.

Photo © Imaginechina

improve environmental conditions, tying the evaluation of local officials to environmental targets, publishing a national climate change policy, and establishing a high-level leadership group to deal with climate change headed by Premier Wen Jiabao.

International Image

China's rapid economic growth has been met with mixed feelings. Some countries view China's development as an opportunity; others feel threatened by the competition. By 2008, China had accumulated a foreign exchange reserve of nearly $2 trillion. While the United States and other Western economies have been pressuring the Chinese government to appreciate its currency as they did in Japan in the 1980s, many economists worry that a sharp rise in the yuan may trigger an economic crisis in China similar to what happened in Japan after the 1985 Plaza Accord. External pressure for currency revaluation has been mounting in light of China's expanding trade surplus, as was the case in Japan in the mid-1980s.

In addition to economic issues, China is also facing serious challenges in its foreign policy and needs a public relations campaign to improve its international image. During the Beijing Olympics torch relay in early 2008, Tibetan and human rights groups protested China's policies toward Tibet, Sudan, and Myanmar. The Olympics was supposed to be China's coming-out party, and the country hoped to use the Olympics to present its best face to the world. But part of the overseas portion of the torch relay was seriously disrupted by all sorts of protestors. What happened before the games was a public relations embarrassment.

An overly negative image abroad could potentially damage China's economy. Eventually, it will be up to China itself to improve its international image. Actions speak louder than words. The Chinese government was praised by many in the West, including some critics, for the way it quickly mobilized to rescue survivors and help with postdisaster reconstruction following the May 2008 earthquake in Sichuan Province. The Chinese government also designated three days of national mourning one week after the earthquake. It was unprecedented in China that the national government led the nation in mourning ordinary citizens who lost their lives in a natural disaster. One hopes that the Chinese government will care not only about the economic growth rate but also about the well-being of the Chinese people.

5

COMPARING EAST ASIAN ECONOMIES

East Asian nations that have managed to succeed since the end of World War II have arguably followed a roughly similar path, with rapid growth occurring under a strong or authoritarian regime, democratization occurring later at higher levels of development, and reforms implemented that are aimed at strengthening existing economic and political institutions. To understand East Asian development models, one has to study the role of the state in shaping the market and vice versa. The East Asian economies did not grow in a vacuum; one also needs to understand how the international political and economic environment shaped East Asia's development. How these economies were affected by and coped with the 1997–98 financial crisis also needs to be studied. However, the East Asian economies did not all follow the same linear pattern. Some features of the economic development of these nations are converging whereas others are diverging.

The state and the market are two central concepts in international political economy. East Asian economies are similar in that they are production oriented, export led, and state directed. They share some of the following major features.

SIMILARITIES

Export-Oriented Policies and "Going Global" Strategies

All the East Asian nations have manufacturing-based trading economies. The export-oriented strategy seemed to be the only realistic route for resource-poor South Korea, Taiwan, and Japan, but the PRC, with richer resources, has also adopted this strategy. It is interesting to compare South Korea, Taiwan, and Japan, which turned their resource paucity into an advantage for development, with developing countries in regions such as Africa, which are suffering from the so-called resource curse despite their abundance of natural resources. *Resource curse* refers to the paradox that countries with an abundance of natural resources tend to have less economic growth than countries without these natural resources. Unlike the case in Africa, the East Asian economies have taken advantage of their strength in human capital and become successful trading powers.

The East Asian economies began to invest and purchase overseas after they had accumulated foreign currency reserves as a result of robust exports. From Japan's purchase of the Rockefeller Center in New York and several Hollywood movie studios to China's purchase of shares in Morgan Stanley and Blackstone and its global investments today, especially in Africa and Latin America, Asian economies are going global and acquiring foreign assets.

Stable Domestic Conditions

Economic development cannot be achieved without a stable political and social environment. All East Asian countries have relatively peaceful and orderly societies. Japan and South Korea enjoyed a long period of domestic stability after World War II and the Korean War. Taiwan's society stabilized after 1950. The island's people had the common goal of "seeking survival and development," and a competitive spirit was instilled in the whole society. With the situation across the Taiwan Strait very confrontational, all residents were especially willing to work together wholeheartedly for economic development. It is therefore little wonder that Taiwan was able to recover so quickly from the ravages of war. The PRC's domestic situation stabilized after Mao's death in 1976 and the end of the Cultural Revolution. Like the others, the PRC began to focus on economic reconstruction after political stability was achieved.

The Active Role of the State

First developed in Japan, developmental state capitalism was widely embraced by the East Asian economies, whose governments actively interacted with markets. The government provided directions for the economy by participating directly or indirectly in basic economic activities, such as building infrastructure and establishing a legal system, and by coordinating or guiding private sector activities.

When the PRC introduced economic reforms in the late 1970s, its political system was intact. The central government or the state machinery was in full control of every provincial and local government in China. Centrally planned practices and institutions were maintained before new market institutions were created. The state fully supported reform initiatives and provided assistance to ensure that they could be carried out smoothly. State policies included maintaining law and order, enforcing rules and regulations, establishing and improving institutional frameworks to suit the new environment, and providing public infrastructure such as roads, schools, and hospitals to the masses. China's strong state and institutional capacity played a crucial role in creating a climate conducive to growth.

State involvement in economic development includes the articulation of national economic goals, the establishment of specialized bureaucracies, the creation of targeted industrial sectors and export-processing zones, and the willingness to thwart popular political resistance. The financial crisis of 1997 facilitated the transformation of a developmental state into a welfare state in South Korea and Japan by bringing social inequality to the forefront of political debate and paving the way for new and more effective welfare policies. The state has also played a very important role in Taiwan's economic development. Before the 1980s, because of the security threat from the PRC, the Taiwanese government had the power to maintain a stable and secure society and strict law and order. This was a necessary condition for both attracting investment and sustaining a good living environment. As tensions with the PRC abated in the 1980s and afterward, the government's authoritarian style was gradually replaced with democratic politics.

To cope with the global economic recession—triggered by the U.S. subprime mortgage crisis that became apparent in 2007—these various Asian governments passed economic stimulus packages in 2008 and 2009. Yet people in these countries are expecting more from their governments, partly because they have become accustomed to active state intervention in the economies. At the beginning of 2009, both Prime Minister Aso Taro of Japan and President Lee Myung-bak of South Korea had very low approval ratings for their ineffective measures to deal with the crisis and were under pressure to resign.

Visionary Individual Leaders

Individuals can shape the course of history. In East Asia, the role of far-sighted leaders such as Yoshida Shigeru, Deng Xiaoping, and Chiang Kai-shek cannot be underestimated in helping their economies take off.

Yoshida's well-designed domestic and foreign policies became the guiding principle of Japan's postwar economic recovery. Chiang Kai-shek strengthened Taiwan's economic base, and his son Chiang Ching-kuo gradually opened up Taiwanese society by allowing the existence of opposition parties, eventually turning Taiwan into a free and prosperous society. "To get rich is glorious,"

坚持党的基本路线一百年不动摇

Pedestrians walk past a big propaganda billboard with the portrait of Deng Xiaoping in Shenzhen city, Guangdong province, January, 2009. The roles played by leaders such as Deng Xiaoping, Yoshida Shigeru, and Chiang Kai-shek in regard to transforming their countries' economies cannot be underestimated. Photo © Imaginechina.

claimed Deng Xiaoping, who encouraged the Chinese to work hard and prosper and introduced privatization policies. In rural areas, the "household responsibility" system was adopted. By the early 1980s, the communes had been disbanded and peasants were given drastically reduced quotas. What food they grew beyond the quota was sold on a free market at unregulated prices. This system was later extended to other sectors of the economy, and local managers were held responsible for the profits and losses of their enterprises. All these leaders had a strong commitment to promoting the well-being of the public.

Investment in Human Resources

Inspiration and perspiration are both needed if a society is to progress. Although cultural determinist views are controversial for their exaggeration of cultural differences and their selective focus on some aspects of a culture, the success of the East Asian countries has been attributed in part to the impact of Confucianism and "Asian values," which include an emphasis on education, hard work, a relatively high level of individual savings due to the lack of adequate welfare measures, a nationalistic desire for a strong state, and a willingness to sacrifice personal interest for the good of society.

Increased productivity is often the result of improvements in education and skills. In both quantity and quality, the East Asian economies have made a major commitment to education and training. For example, in what has been described by the United Nations Educational, Scientific, and Cultural Organization (UNESCO) as "clearly the great experiment in the mass education in the history of the world," literacy rates in China increased from 20 percent in 1949 to 65 percent by the end of the 1970s. China's literacy rate continued to soar as the country began to reopen the economy to the world. In comparison, India's literacy rate stood at 41 percent at the end of the 1970s.[1] A solid educational foundation helps immensely in the absorption of new ideas and the coordination of government policies. As science and technology improved, Taiwan extended compulsory education to nine years in 1968. Meanwhile, additional technological and vocational colleges were established to meet the needs of an industrial sector that was being continuously upgraded. The biggest investment of most families in East Asia is their children's education.

MAJOR DIFFERENCES

Despite the above-mentioned similarities, the development paths of East Asia's economies demonstrate clear differences. These differences are more salient between the PRC and the other three economies.

The External Environment

South Korea and Taiwan are important cases for understanding the role of outside powers. During their authoritarian periods, both South Korea and Taiwan were under American protection. Without the support provided by the U.S. military and American markets, they probably could not have remained independent as late as the early 1980s. The American policy of engagement with these regimes gave the United States the ability to nudge things forward at crucial junctures. The United States was also important as a locus for exiles and a transmitter of ideas and values, and many Taiwanese and Korean leaders studied in the West. The U.S. security umbrella obviously provided an important benefit to Japan, relieving it of the need to fund its own security during the early years of postwar reconstruction. Benign international conditions were extremely conducive to the success of these economies, especially the postwar free trade regime. However, outsiders can only play a role by providing resources, ideas, and strategies. Ultimately it is up to local actors to make democracy work.[2]

While Taiwan and South Korea largely followed Japan's developmental state model, the PRC's growth since the 1970s faced different international political and economic conditions. As the latest developer among the four, the PRC has pursued a more liberal economic policy characterized by relative independence of private businesses rather than statist development strategies. Without security guarantees such as those enjoyed by Japan, South Korea, and Taiwan, the PRC had to build a peaceful regional and international environment for its own economic development. Japanese policies were strongly "antimarket," insulating numerous domestic sectors from international competition and protecting an increasing number of globally noncompetitive firms, such as construction and food processing, at high costs to domestic consumers.[3] Thus, China had to focus on both the international and domestic dimensions whereas the other East Asian economies could largely afford to focus on domestic conditions alone.

Income Distribution

A major feature of the East Asian model is the achievement of high growth with equity. Growth in Japan, South Korea, and Taiwan was attained in tandem with relatively high levels of social and economic equality. High levels economic growth also created a large middle class in these economies, where a civil society emerged and expanded.

By contrast, China's growth has been achieved at the expense of a widening income gap and a worsening of the natural environment. The Chinese middle class remains small and enjoys the status quo. It is unrealistic to rely on the nouveau riche to push for democratization in China. China's trajectory is a departure from other East Asian nations' mixture of high growth with social equality. With its wide discrepancy between rich and poor, China is more like a developing country in regions such as Latin America.

When Deng Xiaoping said "To get rich is glorious," he was encouraging a small minority of the population to become rich, hoping that they would help raise the living standards of the rest of the population. The strategy was only partially successful. A small group has indeed prospered, but most Chinese, especially those living in the vast countryside and inland provinces, remain poor. How to achieve more even development is a major challenge facing China in the twenty-first century.

The PRC Factor

China's economic development exhibits several different features. First, China's economy did not really take off until after 1978, and since then it has developed very rapidly. In just over two decades, China's economy became one of the largest in the world. Second, it has employed a mixture of strategies, including central planning, inward-oriented import-substitution industrialization along with a strong export orientation, and encouragement of foreign direct investment (FDI). Throughout the 1990s and 2000s, the PRC has been the largest recipient of FDI among developing economies. Taiwan and South Korea have also been receptive to FDI. By contrast, Japan has generally resisted it. Third, the PRC has continuously modified its policies, in a creative and innovative manner, in accordance with the prevailing development strategy and the changing domestic and international environment. This was particularly the case in the run-up to and aftermath of its accession to the WTO in 2001.

While it trades extensively with other Asian economies, the PRC has also become a serious competitor with them. The PRC has been remarkably successful in attracting FDI, and foreign-owned firms have been a key driver of the growth of high-value-added Chinese exports. Unlike the Indian diaspora, the Chinese diaspora played a crucial role in providing capital for investment after China initiated its economic reforms in the late 1970s. China established the four special economic zones (SEZs) in the early 1980s on the country's southeast coast, taking advantage of their proximity to Taiwan, Hong Kong, Macao, and Southeast Asia, where large numbers of overseas Chinese were eager to invest in their ancestral homeland. According to Xinhua, its official news agency, in 2007 China attracted $74.77 billion in FDI, an increase of 13.59 percent over the previous year, and ranked first in FDI among developing nations for the fifteenth year in a row.

China's economic growth rate has been around 10 percent for the thirty years since reform policies were introduced in 1978. The Chinese authorities have been struggling to cool down the growth and investment rates in order to deflect inflationary pressures. Since opening its markets to international trade and joining the WTO, China has emerged as a manufacturing powerhouse, playing a central role in the global supply chain for a wide range of products. This process is providing substantial benefits to China and the Asian region in general as China imports components such as computer chips and auto parts from its neighbors for use in its export industries. Of course, China's emergence as a major manufacturing center also poses competitive challenges for its neighbors, which need to adjust to this new feature of the environment.

China's role as a regional manufacturing hub is also leading to significant intraregional investment flows. Large firms in the region, many of them headquartered in South Korea, Taiwan, and Japan, are increasingly moving parts of their production processes to the Chinese mainland. In particular, labor-intensive assembly operations have relocated to take advantage of China's low labor costs. However, as Chinese labor is becoming more expensive, both Chinese and foreign firms are increasingly turning to Vietnam, Bangladesh, and other even lower labor economies.

Other Factors

South Korea's and Japan's economies are large and led by industrial conglomerates while the Taiwanese economy is small and based on family businesses. All are export led, boasting strong information technology (IT) sectors and depending heavily on the U.S. and Chinese markets. Japan, South Korea, and Taiwan had to overcome the obstacle of limited natural resources in rebuilding their war-torn economies. South Korea and Taiwan were in the vanguard when the "third wave" of democratization reached the region in the late 1980s.[4] By the early twenty-first century, both democracies had been consolidated.

The East Asian economies also fared differently during the Asian financial crisis of 1997. What happened in East Asia is not peculiar and had already occurred in many Latin American countries in the 1980s. These economies faced sudden currency depreciations due to speculative attacks or large outflows of funds. The Asian crisis began in Thailand and spread to other Southeast Asian nations before it hit Northeast Asia. South Korea suffered tremendously, and thousands of small and medium-sized companies were plunged into bankruptcy. The International Monetary Fund's short-term macroeconomic policy for Korea was to call for a budget deficit reduction (by raising taxes and cutting government spending) and a tighter monetary policy (with higher interest rates and less credit availability), which together depressed growth and raised unemployment.

The Japanese yen dropped sharply during the financial crisis, causing grave concerns that this would trigger a deeper Asian crisis or world recession. Yet neither the IMF nor Western leaders had asked Japan to increase its interest rate (which at 0.5 percent was among the lowest in the world) to defend the yen. Instead they wanted Japan to take fiscal measures to expand the economy. This tolerance of low interest rates in Japan, as well as pressure on the government to pump up its economy, was a very different approach than the high-interest, austerity-budget medicine prescribed for the other ailing East Asian countries. In the case of the other countries, which owed a great deal to Western banks, the recovery and repayment of their foreign loans was the paramount interest.

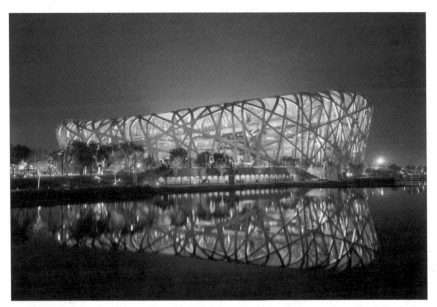

The 2008 Summer Olympics in Beijing—a night view of the National Stadium, known as the "Birds Nest," in Beijing, China, August 2008. Photo © Imaginechina

Helped by their huge foreign exchange reserves, China, Taiwan, and Japan weathered the crisis better than South Korea. In China, whose currency was not freely traded due to tight control by the government, the yuan did not depreciate. As a result, China was barely hit by the financial crisis. It was the rapid buildup of external debt that more than anything else led to the crisis in Thailand, Indonesia, Malaysia, and South Korea. One of the lessons learned is that developing countries should not build up a large foreign debt even if they have relatively large export earnings.

A final interesting comparative point is the question of whether hosting the Olympics can help countries democratize and become fully integrated into the international political and economic system. To a great extent, the 1964 Tokyo Summer Olympics symbolized Japan's formal reentry into the international system where it would play a constructive role. It provided an opportunity to display Japan's industrial and technological achievements to the world, including the new, high-speed, "bullet train" system. The 1988 Seoul Summer Olympics, as with the Tokyo Olympics, served as a catalyst for South Korea's economic development. It also provided an opportunity for South Korea to shake off authoritarian rule and move toward democracy. China staged a spectacular global sporting event in the summer of 2008. Will the summer Olympics do the same for China as it did for Japan and South Korea?

6

TOWARD A COMPREHENSIVE
UNDERSTANDING OF EAST ASIA'S
ECONOMIC "MIRACLES"

East Asian nations made impressive progress in promoting economic growth after World War II. Although each has its unique features, lumped together, they are considered the "East Asian miracle" in international political economy. Other developing regions have yet to discover the secrets of East Asia's success. Although the 1997–98 Asian financial crisis led some people to believe that the miracle was no more than a mirage, East Asia remains one of the most dynamic and prosperous regions in the world, and the average growth rate of these nations is still far higher than those of other regions. While thriftiness is deeply rooted in many Asian cultures and people do save a lot in East Asian countries, their purchasing power cannot be underestimated, even though the rising cost of fuel is affecting the lives of many. One only needs to look at the omnipresent well-to-do tourists from Japan, Taiwan, and South Korea. Even Hawaii and Paris are trying to attract the nouveau riche from China now.

What explains East Asia's economic success? Is the East Asian model sustainable? Professor Paul Krugman of Stanford University argued in 1994 that East Asia's rapid growth in output was nothing extraordinary and could be fully explained by the rapid growth of inputs: expansion of employment, increases in education levels, massive investments in physical capital, and the willingness to save (i.e., to sacrifice current consumption for the sake of future production). These strategies, he suggested, were no different from the Soviet growth model of the 1950s and 1960s.[1]

That the Soviet Union has collapsed and East Asian economies are still very vibrant indicates that the comparison is problematic. Krugman's interpretation of the Soviet miracle is that it was driven by perspiration not inspiration. He mistakenly suggests that Singapore's growth can be explained entirely by increases in measured inputs such as the amount of production and that there is no sign of increased efficiency. This interpretation has also been proven wrong by developments in Japan, South Korea, Taiwan, Hong Kong, and Singapore, as their economies have become high-tech and both productivity and efficiency have greatly improved. Even China, the latest developer among these economies, is focusing on innovation and technological breakthroughs and attempting to build its own brand of automobiles and jumbo passenger airplanes.

A decade after the Asian financial crisis, all of East Asia's economies have strengthened their financial institutions. The experience of Japan in the 1989–92 equity crash and the 1997 financial crisis tells us how costly avoiding financial reforms can be. Failure to recognize and address deep-seated structural problems in the financial sector and governance structure when they first emerged undermined confidence in economic management. This in turn led to a "lost decade" of economic growth. The example of Japan also shows that structural reform remains a necessary condition for sustaining dynamic economic growth even at the most advanced economic level.

One of the key lessons from the Asian financial crisis is that while capital inflows to emerging markets are beneficial for economic development a reversal of capital flows can also occur. Therefore, it is imperative for the emerging economies in Asia and elsewhere to build a financial and legal infrastructure that is resilient to sudden changes in capital flows. Their continued economic success will depend critically on strengthening the institutional framework of the region's economies.[2]

THE STATE AND THE MARKET

Are there secrets to East Asia's continued growth? An emphasis on education, the inclination to save (although Japan's aggregate savings rate has dropped since the 1990s), and an export priority policy seem to be some common strategies adopted by these economies. But there are more. From an international political economy perspective, what are the roles of government and the market in explaining the East Asian success and how has globalization affected development in East Asia?

Scholars and policymakers have reached no consensus on the roles of government and the market in East Asian economic development. Two competing views have shaped inquiries into the source of the rapid growth of East Asian economies and efforts to derive lessons for other developing economies: the market-friendly view, according to which government intervenes little in the market; and the developmental state view, in which the state governs and guides the market. Proponents of the former view see the East Asian story as a vindication of liberal free-market principles, while defenders of the latter view attribute the success of these countries to active and effective government intervention. Interestingly, they share the conception that the market and government are alternative mechanisms for resource allocation in economic development. They are different only in their judgment of the extent to which market failures have been, and ought to be, remedied by direct government intervention. Clearly, both state and market are powerful forces in East Asia's growth.

A third view has been developed by scholars who turn their attention to the way economic decisions were shared and divided between the market and public administration. They recognize that East Asia has strong social capital—social networks among people that can increase productivity both individually and collectively—and institutional foundations for proper development and that the strong role of government or the market might not be the major cause. They have suggested the so-called market-enhancing theory or the synergy between market and government.[3] Instead of viewing government and the market as mutually exclusive substitutes, they examine the capacity of government policy to facilitate or complement private sector coordination. They start from the premise that private sector institutions have important comparative advantages over government, particularly in their ability to quickly process information. At the same time, these analysts recognize that the capabilities of the private sector are limited in developing economies.

There are other explanations for East Asia's spectacular growth. Some scholars have emphasized the role of war in East Asia's development.[4] Wars create states and economies and are powerful agents for political, economic, and social change. These scholars contend that World War II, the Korean War, the Vietnam War, and the constant competition (and preparation for war) between the two Koreas and two Chinas have all stimulated economic growth and social transformations in East Asia. For example, Japan's economy benefited enormously from military procurements during the Korean and Vietnam wars. The Korean War was described by Prime Minister Yoshida Shigeru as "a gift of the gods" in Japan's post–World War II recovery and growth, and large American procurements during the Vietnam War provided additional demand for Japanese goods, which helped sustain the high growth of the 1960s. The almost five-decade Cold War ensured long-term American assistance to and protection of Japan.

The discussion of the economies of East Asia reveals a rich diversity of national systems of political economy in the region. Japan demilitarized and democratized shortly after its surrender at the end of World War II. With the help of the United States, it was quickly integrated into Western political and economic systems. South Korea and Taiwan were authoritarian, military dictatorships when their economies began to take off. As former Japanese colonies, they democratized only after their economies had reached a higher level. The PRC's economic reforms have been overseen by the Communist Party of China. Despite some procedural reforms within the party, including membership for entrepreneurs, China's one-party political structure remains unchanged thirty years after the economic reforms were launched (see Table 6.1)

Table 6.1. Do Political Democracy and
Economic Growth Go Hand in Hand?

	Democracy?	Economic Take-off	Recognized as Democracy
Japan	yes	early 1950s	early 1950s
South Korea	yes	late 1960s	late 1980s
Taiwan	yes	late 1960s	early 1990s
PRC	no	early 1980s	???

In addition to market, state, and war, many other factors have been identified as reasons for East Asia's success—outward policy orientations, high saving and investment rates, an emphasis on achieving and learning, macroeconomic discipline, strong leadership, and external influences—although the relative weight of each in explaining the region's success is still a matter of considerable debate.

LEVELS OF ANALYSIS

To better understand the development trajectories of these East Asian economies, one may also use different levels of analysis to study their performances comparatively. Three levels can be analyzed: international, national (domestic), and individual.

International Conditions

East Asian nations' economic growth is inseparable from the external environment. Generally speaking, the international environment has been conducive to these economies as they attempted to maintain high growth rates. As in other regions, protectionist policies exist in East Asia to shelter domestic industries such as the agricultural sector from international competition. None of these Asian economies chose an isolationist path. Instead, they are very outward looking and welcome international trade and other international exchanges. One can argue that the East Asian economies embraced globalization and have benefited from integration into the global political economy.

On the other hand, the outside world has generally supported and helped these economies to modernize. Japan, South Korea, and Taiwan received valuable political, military, and economic aid from the United States during the early stages of their economic development. The PRC was isolated by the West during much of the Cold War, but later it was assisted in reentering the international community in such matters as membership at the United Nations and WTO. All have had robust trading relations with the West in the past few decades. Japan, South Korea, and Taiwan have also helped the PRC to catch up. All three have invested heavily in the Chinese mainland, and Japan has provided billions of dollars in government loans to China.

An interesting observation is that the Olympics have served as a coming-out party for these nations. From the 1964 summer games in Tokyo to the 1988 summer games in Seoul and the 2008 summer games in Beijing, the Olympics have come to these countries roughly every twenty years, which reflects the fact that their dates of economic takeoff are about twenty years apart.

Domestic Policies

Political stability provided a necessary condition for economic growth. Although politicians in these countries have disagreed on what the best economic policy is and how fast their economies should grow, they have all been committed to promoting economic development and improving living standards.

Beginning in the 1950s, East Asian countries adopted wide-ranging policies aimed at transforming themselves into market economies. Sound macroeconomic policies provided a stable backdrop for business growth. At an early stage, the importance of infrastructure investment as an aid to exporters and import-competing firms was recognized and appropriate measures taken. Later in the reform process greater emphasis was placed on liberalization of the trade and financial sectors. The main thrust of economic policy became an outward orientation with strong incentives for exporters and a commitment to growth through trade.

Individual Leaders

Sound economic policies are determined at the central level of government, often under the leadership of visionary individuals. A national leader must design policies that are most suitable for the nation. More important, these policies have to be effectively implemented, even with an iron hand sometimes.

East Asia is fortunate to have had such individual leaders during the critical years of their economic growth. One can only imagine, without Deng Xiaoping's resolute policy of opening China to the West after Mao's death, how long the country would have struggled in its pursuit of modernization. Likewise, Yoshida Shigeru, Ikeda Hayato, Chiang Kai-shek, Chiang Ching-kuo, Syngman Rhee, and Park Chung-hee all played crucial roles during their countries' economic transformations.

LESSONS FOR OTHER DEVELOPING COUNTRIES

Is there an East Asian development model? This booklet suggests that, although the four economies have some commonalities, their development paths are markedly different. While some attributes are possessed by all, such as an emphasis on education, a relatively high level of savings, and a strong work ethic, these economies have faced different domestic and international challenges; therefore, their policies have been different.

Japan was already an industrial power before World War II. With a solid industrial base, an economy-focused policy, and strong U.S. economic and military support, Japan's postwar recovery, though spectacular, was perhaps not surprising. South Korea and Taiwan followed a similar pattern of development. Protected and prodded by the United States, both designed export-oriented policies and closely linked their growth to the insatiable U.S. market. They confirm the democratization theory that suggests that a country can only move toward democracy when its economic development has reached a certain level. Both formally moved toward democratization in the 1980s after they had achieved impressive economic growth, although they had held elections before.

The situation in the PRC is much more complicated. While sharing some of the development traits of the other three economies, the PRC is much bigger and does not fit any simple model. In fact, there are several Chinas: the coastal China that is quickly catching up with the "Asian tigers" and becoming increasingly cosmopolitan, the rust-belt China of the northeast that reflects the reality and dilemma of many state-owned enterprises in the competitive new economy, and the inland agricultural China that remains poor and underdeveloped.

The East Asian economies did not adopt greater outward orientation according to a common model or blueprint. Only Hong Kong and Singapore have adopted totally free trade policies with virtually no tariff or nontariff barriers. To varying degrees, the other newly industrializing economies (NIEs) in the region all adopted interventionist but market friendly policies, including export promotion and the creation of selective import barriers. These interventionist aspects of trade policy have had great appeal for a number of more recently emerging economies.

East Asia's experience also suggests that political freedom is not a prerequisite for economic growth. The ability of a government to formulate sound economic policies is more important than the type of government. High economic performance will come from both democracies and authoritarian regimes that invest in human capital and physical infrastructure, encourage competition, maintain strong state institutions and legal systems, and adopt consistently sound policies. High savings and investment rates, accumulation of physical and human capital, and market-friendly government policies have all contributed to East Asia's success.

Many analysts, including Joseph Stiglitz—the Columbia University economics professor and former Senior Vice President and Chief Economist of the World Bank—argue that government intervention has played a critical role in East Asia's economic success. Governments in East Asia used industrial policies to affect the allocation of resources in ways that would stimulate economic growth. They took an entrepreneurial role in identifying industries in which research and development would have high payoffs. These governments intervened actively in the market; they used, complemented, regulated, and indeed created markets rather than supplanting them. They created an environment in which markets could thrive. These governments promoted exports, education, and technology; encouraged cooperation between government and industry and between firms and their workers; and at the same time, at least in some important sectors such as automobiles and electronics, encouraged competition. No single policy ensured success, nor did the absence of any single ingredient ensure failure. Why did governments undertake these policies? Why did politicians or bureaucrats not subvert them for their own self-interest? "The real miracle of East Asia may be more political than economic," Stiglitz claims.[5]

East Asia was not the favored candidate for rapid economic growth during the 1950s. It had too many people and too few resources. Most observers favored the resource-rich African countries that were then moving towards independence. East Asia's development experience suggests that it is possible to catch up. Developing countries can move up the ladder. East Asia's experience is also a testament to the fact that countries with an authoritarian past can find a path to economic prosperity and democratic transition and consolidation.

As successful as they are, East Asian economies are not immune to global economic crises. High savings rates in these nations have been considered one of the "secrets" to their success, but now East Asians are encouraged to spend more to stimulate domestic growth. As the economic recession spread to the region in 2008 and 2009, East Asian governments were being criticized by the West for not promoting domestic consumption despite the fact that cash had been distributed by some of these governments to encourage spending.

The 2008–09 economic slump in East Asia also exposes the vulnerability of export-dependent economies. As cash-strapped Americans and Europeans decrease their demand for consumer goods, export sectors in East Asia have suffered tremendously. In the first half of 2008 alone, 67,000 small and medium-sized export-focused businesses were forced to close in China. Yet, many Asians remain optimistic. While visiting a factory in January 2009, Premier Wen Jiabao of China expressed his confidence that China was determined to be the first major economy to recover from the global downturn.

Not all roads lead to Rome. Developing countries that attempt to imitate East Asia's success may have to seek a development path most suitable for themselves based on their own histories, cultures, societies, and domestic and international environments. Which aspects of the East Asian "miracles" will work for other countries must be determined through pragmatic experimentation and adaptation based on local conditions.

NOTES

CHAPTER 2

[1] Ezra F. Vogel, *Japan as Number One: Lessons for America* (Cambridge, MA: Harvard University Press, 1979).

[2] Ming Wan, *The Political Economy of East Asia: Striving for Wealth and Power* (Washington, DC: Congressional Quarterly Press, 2008), 27.

[3] http://en.wikipedia.org/wiki/Ikeda_Hayato.

[4] Chalmers Johnson, *MITI and the Japanese Miracle: The Growth of Industrial Policy 1925–1975* (Stanford, CA: Stanford University Press, 1982).

[5] See T. J. Pemple, *Regime Shift: Comparative Dynamics of the Japanese Political Economy* (Ithaca, NY: Cornell University Press, 1998); Richard Katz, *Japan, the System That Soured: The Rise and Fall of the Japanese Economic Miracle* (Armonk, NY: M. E. Sharpe, 1998); and Meredith Woo-Cumings, ed., *The Developmental State* (Ithaca, NY: Cornell University Press, 1999).

[6] "U.S. Occupation Assistance: Iraq, Germany, and Japan Compared," Congressional Research Service, Library of Congress, Washington, DC, March 23, 2006.

[7] The Plaza Accord (or Plaza Agreement) was an agreement signed on September 22, 1985, at the Plaza Hotel in New York City by the ministers of finance and central bank governors of five nations: France, West Germany, Japan, the United States, and the United Kingdom. These five economies agreed to, among other things, depreciate the U.S. dollar in relation to the Japanese yen and German deutsche mark by intervening in currency markets. The exchange-rate value of the dollar versus the yen declined by 51 percent over the next two years. The signing of the Plaza Accord signified Japan's emergence as a real player in the global economy and the international monetary system.

[8] James R. Martin, "World Competitiveness Reports Summary," http://maaw.info/WorldCompetitivenessReports.htm; Ezra Vogel, *Is Japan Still Number One?* (Suban Jaya, Malaysia: Pelanduk Publications, 2001).

[9] "Japanese Economy Not First Class, Says Minister," *Times* (London), January 19, 2008.

[10] Edward J. Lincoln, "The Japanese Government and the Economy: Twenty-first Century Challenges," *Education About Asia* 12, no. 3 (winter 2007): 31–38.

CHAPTER 3

[1] Kwan S. Kim, "The Korean Miracle (1962–1980) Revisited: Myths and Realities in Strategy and Development," Working Papers, no. 166, University of Notre Dame, November 1991.

[2] Seymour Martin Lipset, "Some Social Requisites of Democracy: Economic Development and Political Legitimacy," *American Political Science Review* 53, no. 1 (March 1959): 69–105; Samuel P. Huntington, *Political Order in Changing Societies* (New Haven, CT: Yale University Press, 1968).

[3] David C. Kang, *Crony Capitalism: Corruption and Development in South Korea and the Philippines* (New York, NY: Cambridge University Press, 2002).

[4] Hagen Koo, ed., *State and Society in Contemporary Korea* (Ithaca, NY: Cornell University Press, 1993).

CHAPTER 4

[1] Thomas B. Gold, *State and Society in the Taiwan Miracle* (Armonk, NY: M. E. Sharpe, 1986), 125–26.

[2] Government Information Office, "The Story of Taiwan: Economy," www.taiwan.com.au/Polieco/History/ROC/report04.html (May 1, 2008). The Gini coefficient is a statistical measure of inequality of income distribution. It is defined as a ratio with values between zero and 1. A low Gini coefficient indicates more equal income or wealth distribution, while a high one indicates more unequal distribution. Zero corresponds to perfect equality (where everyone has the same income), and 1 corresponds to perfect inequality (where one person has all the income and everyone else has none).

[3] These three paragraphs are adapted from "Key Issues in China's Economic Transformation," United Nations Conference on Trade and Development (UNCTAD), www.unctad.org, accessed on March 24, 2008.

[4] Orville Schell, "The Enigma of China's Economic 'Miracle,'" *AsiaMedia*, November 1, 2003.

CHAPTER 5

[1] "China's Miracle," *Star* (Malaysia), March 20, 2008.

[2] Tom Ginsburg, "Democratic Transitions: Case Studies from Asia," *Foreign Policy Research Institute E-Notes*, http://www.fpri.org, December 19, 2007.

[3] T. J. Pempel, "Revisiting the Japanese Economic Model," in *Japan and China in the World Political Economy*, edited by Saadia M. Pekkanen and Kellee S. Tsai (London and New York: Routledge, 2005), 35–36.

[4] Political scientist Samuel P. Huntington in *The Third Wave: Democratization in the Late Twentieth Century* (Norman, OK: University of Oklahoma Press, 1993), used the term "the third wave of democratization" to refer to the global trend between 1974 and 1990 when approximately thirty countries, from Southern and Eastern Europe to Latin America and Asia, made the transition to democracy. The first wave brought democracy to Western Europe and North America in the eighteenth and nineteenth centuries. The second wave began after World War II but lost steam in the 1960s.

CHAPTER 6

[1] Paul Krugman, "The Myth of Asia's Miracle," *Foreign Affairs* 73, no. 6 (November–December 1994): 62–78.

[2] Takatoshi Kato, "Can the East Asian Miracle Persist?" Speech delivered at Princeton University, December 2, 2004.

[3] Masahiko Aoki et al., eds., *The Role of Government in East Asian Economic Development: Comparative Institutional Analysis* (New York, NY: Oxford University Press, 1998); Robert Wade, *Governing the Market: Economic Theory and the Role of Government in East Asian Industrialization* (Princeton, NJ: Princeton University Press, 2003).

[4] Richard Stubbs, *Rethinking Asia's Economic Miracle* (New York: Palgrave-Macmillan, 2005).The American sociologist and political scientist Charles Tilly first proposed the thesis that states make war and wars make states in *Coercion, Capital, and European States: A.D. 990–1992* (Malden, MA: Blackwell, 1993).

[5] Joseph Stiglitz, "Some Lessons from the East Asian Miracle," *World Bank Research Observer* 11, no. 2 (August 1996): 175.

Suggestions for Further Reading

Adams, F. Gerard, and Shinichi Ichimura, eds. *East Asian Development: Will the East Asian Miracle Growth Survive?* Westport, CT: Praeger, 1998.

Amsden, Alice. *Asia's Next Giant: South Korea and the Late Industrialization.* Oxford: Oxford University Press, 1989.

Amyx, Jennifer A. *Japan's Financial Crisis: Institutional Rigidity and Reluctant Change.* Princeton: Princeton University Press, 2004.

Aoki, Masahiko, Hyung-Ki Kim, and Masahiro Okuno-Fujiwara, eds. *The Role of Government in East Asian Economic Development: Comparative Institutional Analysis.* Oxford: Oxford University Press, 1998.

Bende-Nabende, Anthony, ed. *International Trade, Capital Flows, and Economic Development in East Asia: The Challenge in the Twenty-first Century.* Hampshire: Ashgate, 2003.

Berger, Peter L., and Michael Hsin-huang Hsiao, eds. *In Search of an East Asian Development Model.* New Brunswick, NJ: Transaction, 1988.

Brødsgaard, Kjeld Erik, and Susan Young, eds. *State Capacity in East Asia: Japan, Taiwan, China, and Vietnam.* New York: Oxford University Press, 2000.

Chan, Steve, Cal Clark, and Danny Lam, eds. *Beyond the Developmental State: East Asia's Political Economies Reconsidered.* New York: St. Martin's, 1998.

Chang, Ha-Joon. *The East Asian Development Experience: The Miracle, the Crisis, and the Future.* London and New York: Zed, 2007.

Cohen, Warren I. *East Asia at the Center: Four Thousand Years of Engagement with the World.* New York: Columbia University Press, 2000.

Dickson, Bruce J. *Democratization in China and Taiwan: The Adaptability of Leninist Parties.* New York: Oxford University Press, 1997.

————. *Red Capitalists in China: The Party, Private Entrepreneurs, and Prospects for Political Change*. New York: Columbia University Press, 2003.

Drysdale, Peter. *Reform and Recovery in East Asia: The Role of the State and Economic Enterprise*. London and New York: Routledge, 2000.

Flynn, Norman. *Miracle to Meltdown in Asia: Business, Government, and Society*. Oxford: Oxford University Press, 1999.

Forsberg, Aaron. *America and the Japanese Miracle: The Cold War Context of Japan's Postwar Economic Revival, 1950–1960*. Chapel Hill: University of North Carolina Press, 2000.

Ginsburg, Tom. "Democratic Transitions: Case Studies from Asia." *Foreign Policy Research Institute E-Notes*, http://www.fpri.org, December 1, 2007.

Glick, Reuven, and Ramon Moreno. "The East Asian Miracle: Growth Because of Government Intervention and Protectionism or in Spite of It?" *Business Economics*, Vol. 32:2 (April 1997): 20–25.

Gold, Thomas B. *State and Society in the Taiwan Miracle*. Armonk, NY: M. E. Sharpe, 1986.

Goldstein, Morris. *The Asian Financial Crisis: Causes, Cures, and Systemic Implications*. Washington, DC: Institute for International Economics, 1998.

Haggard, Stephan. *Pathways from the Periphery: Politics of Growth in the Newly Industrializing Countries*. Ithaca: Cornell University Press, 1990.

Harrison, Lawrence E., and Samuel P. Huntington, eds. *Culture Matters: How Values Shape Human Progress*. New York: Basic Books, 2000.

Hira, Anil. *An East Asian Model for Latin American Success: The New Path*. Hampshire: Ashgate, 2007.

Hsueh, Li-min, Chen-kuo Hsu, and Dwight H. Perkins. *Industrialization and the State: The Changing Role of the Taiwan Government in the Economy, 1945–1998*. Cambridge: Harvard Institute for International Development, 2001.

Huang, Yasheng. *Selling China: Foreign Direct Investment during the Reform Era*. Cambridge: Cambridge University Press, 2003.

Hughes, Helen, ed. *Achieving Industrialization in East Asia*. Cambridge: Cambridge University Press, 1988.

Ikeo, Aiko. *Economic Development in Twentieth-Century East Asia: The International Context.* London and New York: Routledge, 1997.

Islam, Iyanatul, and Anis Chowdhury. *The Political Economy of East Asia: Post-Crisis Debates.* Oxford: Oxford University Press, 2000.

Ito, Takatoshi, and Anne O. Krueger, eds. *Growth Theories in Light of the East Asian Experience.* Chicago: University of Chicago Press, 1995.

————. *The Role of Foreign Direct Investment in East Asian Economic Development.* Chicago: University of Chicago Press, 2000.

Jackson, Karl D., ed. Asian Contagion: *The Causes and Consequences of a Financial Crisis.* Boulder: Westview, 1999.

Johnson, Chalmers. *MITI and the Japanese Miracle: The Growth of Industrial Policy, 1925–1975.* Stanford: Stanford University Press, 1982.

Kang, David C. *Crony Capitalism: Corruption and Development in South Korea and the Philippines.* New York: Cambridge University Press, 2002.

Kato, Takatoshi. "Can the East Asian Miracle Persist?" Speech delivered at Princeton University, December 2, 2004; http://www.imf.org/external/np/speeches/2004/120204.htm.

Katz, Richard. Japan: *The System That Soured—the Rise and Fall of the Japanese Economic Miracle.* Armonk, NY: M. E. Sharpe, 1998.

————. *Japanese Phoenix: The Long Road to Economic Revival.* Armonk, NY: M. E. Sharpe, 2002.

Katzenstein, Peter. *A World of Regions: Asia and Europe in the American Imperium.* Ithaca: Cornell University Press, 2005.

Kim, Kwan S. "The Korean Miracle (1962–1980) Revisited: Myths and Realities in Strategy and Development." Working Papers, no. 166, University of Notre Dame, November 1991.

Kim, Samuel S., ed. *East Asia and Globalization.* Lanham, MD: Rowman and Littlefield, 2000.

Koo, Hagen, ed. *State and Society in Contemporary Korea.* Ithaca: Cornell University Press, 1993.

Krugman, Paul. "The Myth of Asia's Miracle." *Foreign Affairs* 73, no. 6 (November–December 1994): 62–78.

Lee, Kuan Yew. *The Singapore Story: Memoirs of Lee Kuan Yew.* Singapore: Prentice Hall, 1998.

Lee, You-Il. *From Evolution to Revolution: Korea's New Market Environment.* Hampshire: Ashgate, 2003.

Lin, Justin Yifu, Fang Cai, and Zhou Li. *The China Miracle: Development Strategy and Economic Reform.* Hong Kong: Chinese University Press, 1996.

Lipset, Seymour Martin. "Some Social Requisites of Democracy: Economic Development and Political Legitimacy." *American Political Science Review* 53, no. 1 (March 1959): 69–105.

Nissanke, Machiko, and Ernest Aryeetey, eds. *Comparative Development Experiences of Sub-Saharan Africa and East Asia: An Institutional Approach.* Hampshire: Ashgate, 2003.

Pei, Minxin. *China's Trapped Transition: The Limits of Developmental Autocracy.* Cambridge: Harvard University Press, 2006.

Pekkanen, Saadia M., and Kellee S. Tsai, eds. *Japan and China in the World Political Economy.* London and New York: Routledge, 2005.

Pempel, T. J. *Regime Shift: Comparative Dynamics of the Japanese Political Economy.* Ithaca: Cornell University Press, 1998.

———. *The Politics of the Asian Economic Crisis.* Ithaca: Cornell University Press, 1999.

Pempel, T. J., ed. *Remapping East Asia: The Construction of a Region.* Ithaca: Cornell University Press, 2004.

Petri, Peter A. *The Lessons of East Asia: Common Foundations of East Asian Success.* Washington, DC: World Bank, 1993.

Przeworski, Adam. *States and Markets: A Primer in Political Economy.* Cambridge: Cambridge University Press, 2003.

Ramo, Joshua Cooper. *The Beijing Consensus.* London: Foreign Policy Center, 2004.

Schell, Orville. "The Enigma of China's Economic 'Miracle.'" *AsiaMedia* (UCLA Asia Institute), November 1, 2003.

Stiglitz, Joseph. "Some Lessons from the East Asian Miracle." *World Bank Research Observer* 11, no. 2 (August 1996): 151–77.

Stiglitz, Joseph, and Shahid Yusuf. *Rethinking the East Asian Miracle.* Washington, DC: World Bank, 2001.

Stubbs, Richard. *Rethinking Asia's Economic Miracle.* New York: Palgrave-Macmillan, 2005.

Sugihara, Kaoru, ed. Japan, *China, and the Growth of the Asian International Political Economy, 1850–1949.* Oxford: Oxford University Press, 2005.

Tilly, Charles. *Coercion, Capital, and European States, A.D. 990–1992.* Malden, MA: Blackwell, 1993.

Vogel, Ezra. *Japan as Number One: Lessons for America.* Cambridge: Harvard University Press, 1979.

———. *Is Japan Still Number One?* Suban Jaya: Pelanduk, 2001.

Vogel, Steven K. *Japan Remodeled: How Government and Industry Are Reforming Japanese Capitalism.* Ithaca: Cornell University Press, 2006.

Wade, Robert. *Governing the Market: Economic Theory and the Role of Government in East Asian Industrialization.* Princeton: Princeton University Press, 2003.

Wan, Ming. *The Political Economy of East Asia: Striving for Wealth and Power.* Washington, DC: Congressional Quarterly Press, 2008.

Wang, Shaoguang, and Angang Hu. *The Political Economy of Uneven Development: The Case of China.* Armonk, NY: M. E. Sharpe, 1999.

Whang, I-J. "The Role of Government in Economic Development: The Korean Experience." *Asian Development Review* 5, no. 2 (1987): 70–87.

Woo-Cumings, Meredith, ed. *The Developmental State.* Ithaca: Cornell University Press, 1999.

World Bank. *East Asia: Recovery and Beyond.* Washington, DC: World Bank, 2000.

Zoellick, Robert. "Economics and Security in the Changing Asia-Pacific." *Survival* 39, no. 4 (winter 1997–98): 29–51.